THE STRENGTH
IN THE LIFE OF
AN EX-MILITARY WIFE

Kimberly Blake

ISBN: 978-0-578-33838-5

Interior and Cover Designed by TWA Solutions.com

Disclaimer:
The information provided in this book is designed to provide helpful information on the subjects discussed. This book is not meant to be used, nor should it be used, for legal advice. Please consult an attorney for legal advice. The publisher and author are not responsible for any specific legal action that may require an attorney and are not liable for any damages or negative consequences from any legal consequences, to any person reading or following the information in this book. References are provided for informational purposes only and do not constitute an endorsement of any websites or other sources. Readers should be aware that the websites listed in this book may change.

Dedication

To God...

For blessing me with the talents and gifts You chose for me. Even when I'm not worthy, You give me sufficient grace. Thank you for loving me despite my flaws and my imperfections because you are *Love*. Thank you, Lord, for pouring Your patience, kindness, and forgiveness, along with a loving heart, into my spirit and soul. Through You, I know all things are possible even when it seems uncomfortable. You kept me when I couldn't keep myself.

Many times, I thought I'd lose breath with the obstacles that I'd faced. Lord, I know You said that if I didn't trust you with these trials, I would groan in the wilderness, but you knew my strength. You knew what the outcome would be for me. You knew that everything I faced would strengthen me, make me wiser, and more educated to bring forth and birth a whole new me with a different mindset.

I give you all the praise and glory for this opportunity to birth this book. I love you, Lord, and thanks for listening to me every morning, noon, and night when I talked to you.

To military wives...

You carry the stripes, too. Metaphorically speaking, you are on the front lines of the battlefield. You are always on duty. You stand for the red, white, and blue, which comes with the blood, sweat, and tears of the meanings behind it. You, too, are the true "Active Military" soldiers, sailors, and marines in my eyes. You continue to hold down the fort!

You are the foundation behind the success of our military men and women who serve this country. Let no one tell you any different. You deal with the agony of separation and the grieving of loved ones lost. In the middle of the night, you pray God will make or break a situation that no one else knows about in dealing with this type of life. You have worn your masks, whether happy or sad, with dignity, involuntarily or voluntarily.

I have so much respect for you because I've lived your life. I have so much respect for wives of civilian men that you've loved through your souls. I know that love all too well. You are God's daughters and you are treasured.

To my newfound friends of the Women's Group…

I involuntarily attended anger management classes in Building U-111 on the Norfolk Naval Base in Norfolk, Virginia. There, I connected with Shenora, Esther, Stephanie, Makala, Heidi, Maranda, Ebony, Michelle, and Patricia. Ladies, thank you for sharing all your stories. Initially, the thought of joining such a group was appalling and beneath me. I didn't think I would have anything in common with anyone. However, it was a blessing in disguise. Sometimes, God knows just where to send you and what you need to hear to open your eyes. I learned that my problem was not only about my spouse but about me. That if I allow someone to dictate who I am and believe them, it makes it all that much truer and I'll lose myself. I don't have to react to anyone's actions, I have total control over the choices I make. I need to make changes internally if I want to change my life.

We had stories filled with broken promises, broken hearts, mistrust, violence, and misunderstandings because of the miscommunications between ourselves and others. However, remember to put God first, you, and then your situation. You are never alone in whatever storms that cross your paths. You are conquerors, in Jesus' name. I wish you all the best of luck and I pray God will dwell in your households with or without someone else to guide you in the right direction because He is all you need. I will never forget you. You have become a part of my life and guidance in my future. I love you all.

To you, the reader…

You are a special type of woman who defines strength in more than a million ways.

So here it is… This is my chance to give something back from my journey.

Acknowledgments

To my two beautiful children...

I cherish your souls with everything I have. I love you unconditionally, with all my heart and soul. You are my strength and you keep me going when I've wanted to give up. Because of you, I know what sacrifice means when you love someone. Because of you, I've learned what priorities mean. You have taught me to search within myself so much more. I've learned that under no circumstances, God is first and to seek Him first on every decision I make. Because of you, I've learned that if it's not broken, don't fix it. You have taught me to stay faithful to what was instilled in me all along—be me instead of trying to step outside of who God made me. I've learned a great deal from you and for that, I thank you so very much.

I'd look at your faces and know that you are the reasons God spared my life through the birth of you, my precious daughter, and during my pregnancy with you, my handsome son. There is no honor greater than being your mother. I thank God for allowing me the opportunity to love and nurture you for the time that was given to me to do so. As a mom, it's always hard to let go of the bicycle to watch you pedal with no training wheels because you are a part of me. We will always have an unbreakable bond.

I love you with every breath that I take and pray for you to stay on the path toward greatness, prosperity, humbleness, forgiveness, endurance, seeking God, loving and praying for one another and that your lives are abundantly blessed. Love you...

To my mother…

You told me I shouldn't give up my dream and to reach out to those who didn't know my story. I love you and thank you for your encouraging me to finish this book. There were many days when we were on the phone and you said good would come from this. I heard you, Mom, but the enemy was busy, telling me I couldn't do this. Telling me it was beyond my reach. Telling me my body was numb, tired, and I had no motivation to move forward. Still, your words stuck in my head, to keep the goal and turn it into an accomplishment. Thanks for being my mother.

To my sister and brother—you are stuck with me forever— and my old friends and new…

I love you all and will forever be grateful for your being in my life.

To everyone else I have not mentioned, I acknowledge you, too. Those that I have met and have had a great time with during the season that you have been in my life, I appreciate you for being a part of my life journey.

For the things that I have experienced in my lifetime and the people that I have had the pleasure of crossing paths with through just saying hello to or them leaving a wise gesture to me to help my spirit, I am most grateful to God for putting those people in my life. I have had a wonderful life and beautiful people in it. I can't ask for much more besides asking Him to keep on blessing me, even in my trials. I am truly honored, grateful, and blessed.

Acknowledgments

To my editor, Jessica Tilles

I can't thank God enough for aligning the people He did on my journey to lead me to you. Throughout this whole ordeal, the biggest fears I had in completing this book were calmed by your encouragement, lessons, trustworthiness, and personable personality. You were available when called upon for questions and down-to-earth, along with honesty regarding various parts of this book.

There are so many things I've learned in writing and keeping things clear and precise for the audience to grasp and visualize all that I'd experienced. Your skills in cleaning up words and saying exactly what it was I was trying to say have blown me out of the water. Thank you so much for blessing me with your years of talent and professionalism. I know we've spoken many times over the phone, but one day I am determined to meet face-to-face with the woman that made this possible. You have made it possible for me to inspire and reach women all over the world by telling my story and giving helpful information that I wasn't given during my storms.

Because you knew the underlying purpose of it all was to release, forgive, heal and help, you understood that it was not to bash, vent in anger, or point fingers because it's all in the past and to speak about it and let go allowed things to flourish into this wonderful masterpiece. I am more than grateful, thankful, and humbled to have you in my life. You are stuck with me!

INTRODUCTION

The Strength in the Life of an Ex-military Wife is for women who can relate to hardships, separations, heartache, misunderstandings, deception, truths, lies, compromises, disappointments, backbiting, slander, betrayal, and forgiveness.

It is for those who have gone through or are enduring turmoil, numbness, confusion, degradation, humiliation, bitterness, embarrassment, being torn, brokenness, one step short of a nervous breakdown, and trying to find a breakthrough in healing from an open wound.

After all the trials and tribulations I've gone through, I'm still standing and dancing in the rain and occasional thunderstorm, and you will, too. This book is about being protected during hurricanes. Jesus not only did this for me as I came to Him a wreck and clueless, but He had to break me from things in my thinking and decision making. God had to get me to where there was no one else I could reach out to outside of Him during my dark hours.

There is much to be said about the different avenues married couples take in life but a married couple in the military gives the word *commitment* a whole new meaning. To be affiliated with this lifestyle and watch my life dramatically change after said commitment showed me that what I thought was commitment turned into hard decisions and what seemed like a lifelong tragedy after deciding to walk away.

I'd driven myself to the point of losing my mind when suddenly God put it on my heart that I didn't have to go through this. God said the only person who could maneuver the direction I was to go was Him, but I needed to get out of the driver's seat to let Him steer. He told me that going crazy and trying to fight with my mouth, the only tool I felt I had to defend my honor, was not how He would have it to be. I was to put God first, then my marriage. I remember Him saying to me He would walk with me as I backtracked through my marriage to not only see the faults of others but my own as well. I cried endlessly after hearing those words and dealing with it being so hard to *let go and let God*. Seeing my faults was hard, but fair. It stung and allowed me to grow in the end.

Times were hard during this process and as I remained silent during my hurt, I confronted things, but accepted apologies, even though I knew in my heart it would happen again. Over other things, I thought my role was to submit. I'd tried it, but it wasn't enough.

To love, cherish, and honor were all placed in different spots and scattered around the world as things crumbled and felt like a *Lifetime* movie, yet very real.

I found out that there was no longer a team of two but a team of thousands and I no longer had my well-deserved post as being *the one*. I learned and lived the saying, "Your family doesn't come in your seabag." Once he boarded the ship, we separated mentally, emotionally, and physically. I learned the affiliation with the military meant the immediate family was one thing and that the competition was against a family of millions, which were people you had an attachment to, but may never meet.

The men in the military serve our country. Dedication and commitment are about the oath of being nominated for such a job that is to protect our country and the people in it, but the closest people to the ones who oversee protecting this country are in a war unprotected. I was constantly trying to understand how one could protect and handle with care a nation when the immediate family was in desperate need of provisions.

Anger and not understanding the hurt consumed me. My marriage was to be forever and stand the test of time. How could this have happened to me? What happened that made him choose to confide, commit, and please someone else? These questions, among so many others, constantly swam around with no answers. My children couldn't help me because they were, of course, not equipped to deal with my issues, and why would they? They didn't ask to become a part of such disarray. My friends from home couldn't help outside of consoling me and, although I appreciated it, it wasn't enough. My mother couldn't help me because I kept so many things from her for fear she would form an opinion about my marriage, and I wanted to prove I could handle my life. So, when the world was asleep, I couldn't call anyone but God.

I went through some terrible things and I don't know how I survived what seemed like a heart attack once my heart had truly broken. But I did.

"He heals the brokenhearted and binds up their wounds."
–Psalm 147:3

Once I healed I was free. Although it was a long journey for me to get here, I look back at that place and am thankful for it because I learned life, marriage, pain, strength, and growth. I learned that I have the power to rewrite my entire life and my comings and goings. Was I not my own individual? I was but had forgotten once I became a wife and mother. I'd listen to the opinions of others, telling me what they would do if it were their situation. "Girl, you are crazy if you stay a minute longer," one person told me. All these different voices had solutions to what would only affect *my* life in the end. I had to do what I needed to do and I was the one who had to face my own decisions. It came with a price and I paid for it.

My grandmother once said, "Kim, marriage isn't easy, but if you love that person, you just don't give up without trying everything there is to try to make sure that's really what you want to do. You have to talk to each other and stop all of that fighting because it will get you nowhere fast. You've got a beautiful family, but you've got to learn how to deal with each other." I listened to every word, but how many of us feel that when our marriages are on the rocks, it seems we are the ones to get all the advice and spiritual wisdom? Have you ever felt like saying, "I hear everything you are saying to me, but when is someone going to tell him this?" It was hard, but it was what I'd chosen and then left.

Time wasn't my friend while intending to get to the other end, but all that time I'd dealt with the trials was important because, without it, I would have never seen me for me. It gets better, and no one may tell you how long it should take because everyone's healing is different. For some, it may take two to six months to get over it. For others, it takes much longer to move forward for fear of things happening again. For some, it's a never healing thing, much like losing a loved one and nothing is left but that pain. Sometimes people never get over heartbreak, and all they hold on to is bitterness. For some, this is easier to do than to move on. This I know all too well.

Before *The Strength in the Life of an Ex-military Wife* became a book, it was my journal that I spent shedding many late-night tears while my children were fast asleep. So much was happening in my life. I got carpal tunnel from writing so much. It was my venting, my scapegoat, my form of personal counseling, so I could stay in my marriage. I strived to stand my ground, to stick it out. I didn't want to abandon ship because the going got tough. God didn't promise a bed of roses in marriage, for He said there would be trials and tribulations so I was gearing up. Writing to release some smoke became too much as the smoke became too thick and my cough turned into straight choking.

Everyone has a story, whether they share it on paper or by word of mouth. They have the right to get it off their chest. There is always a way to share without bashing. This isn't what my book is about. It is about truths and letting go of memories that haunted me for years and I couldn't share. It is about releasing the hurt of what was unfairly and unnecessarily done to me. My heart was open to friendship, co-parenting, and a great relationship because I wanted to show my children the possibilities after a broken home.

I needed to share not with bad intentions because I forgave, but with the right to heal from what I'd gone through. It became my goal to testify to an unfortunate turn of events that turned fortunate in the end. This was a strength birthed from a place I never knew existed in me. A strength that overtook me when I was going to lose my mind. My strength displayed the equivalent of a million elephants' weight that I never knew I had. Courage through my strength during a lifetime of growth and experiences that only I can tell. This was my strength in the life of becoming an ex-military wife.

I pray it finds you well-fed mentally, spiritually, and physically. I speak into existence healing, abundance, provision, growth, and victory over your lives as the beautiful women that God created you to be. I have always been a conqueror, just had to find it. You are conquerors, too.

CHAPTER ONE

Truths Came Home to Me *One by One*

So many times, we see truths but turn a blind eye. Thinking or hoping it was a figment of our imaginations or simply a lie about what's right in front of us.

I went through this for years, looking past glimpses of distrust and wanting to give things a chance. Relationships are hard this way. I didn't want to run at the first sight of trials and tribulations or give up so easily. Everyone has their flaws. No one is perfect, so we wait it out. Love, too much time invested, not wanting to start all over, and feeling at least we know the person's downfalls become reasons for staying. Who wants to do this again with someone new? This is the hesitant reason for walking away when there is mistrust.

It seemed to always be something, and I continued to cover it, allowing others to feel that the issue was with me. I wore my masks voluntarily and involuntarily, but I wore them still. I wasn't ready to wave the flag of defeat. This was my marriage. I believed we could change things around, even if it was against the odds.

I faced ridicule and people talked about me. I was unwelcomed from the beginning because of issues of their own. People hurled accusations of my being barren simply because I was not conceiving within the timeframe they felt was appropriate. "Maybe you can adopt," one person said. I told them, "I don't need to adopt. It will happen when God means for it to happen." You can only look idiocy in the eye and feel for them and say what you need to say within respectful boundaries because of your attachment. I thought, *The nerve of ignorance*. Still, it haunted me to hear my femininity questioned.

In the house we lived in before becoming a part of the military life, our kitchen had a huge closet outside of the other cupboards and pantries. I made it my prayer closet, where daily I prayed to have a child because I felt the pressure around me and the looks along with the questions over when we would start a family. I was young then and wasn't as strong-willed. I allowed others to affect my strength and would cry out to God daily to touch my womb. I had tests that were unnecessary procedures through my naval from them seeing scar tissue in my tubes after depositing painful dye inside me and determining that this caused my not getting pregnant. Only to go back after the test to see that all the scar tissue had disappeared. I believe it was because my pastor at the time had prayed over me, while placing her hand on my stomach, and the power of God was the reason behind this.

This proved to me that God was listening, and He'd heard me. It was going to happen, but not in my time, but his. I was around camouflaged *faith* and backstabbing actions, along with manipulating characters that had full blankets pulled over everyone's eyes. What a beginning it was, but it was the choice I made, and I wasn't backing down from it.

When I was pregnant with my daughter, we'd agreed to join the military life to make things better after so many interruptions in our lives. I'd separated myself from the marriage and this was the resolution, so we left and entered a whole new world. He promised a different bond. He promised it would be just us and our new addition. Again, we were young. No counseling before marriage, no true spiritual input of whether we were ready for such an important step. We did what we both wanted to do and agreed that leaving was best if we were going to dwell without interceptions.

Things were exciting living a new, foreign life—meeting new people, seeing different parts of the world, learning how things go in this life called the military, and setting up housing and learning all the logos that go with the territory.

It's a life that's co-ed and a life I would soon find out how even more sorted and separated I'd become from our mutual agreement.

I was into my ninth month of pregnancy and, let's just say, my size was equivalent to the Michelin Man. We'd been in our new place for a bit and the first couple we met, the wife was very standoffish and wasn't friendly toward me. She wasn't interested in getting to know me, that much was clear. Later, after warming up to her—I needed someone to at least talk to—she told me she'd dealt with things she never thought she would have to in this life and was very hurt and scarred behind it. She had no trust in other women around her spouse and was still in the stages of healing and forgiving. They'd been in for a few years and she had enough experience that led her not to have too much trust in others.

Even though I hadn't experienced her journey, I empathized with her and prayed I wouldn't become her.

We didn't have a car so we were searching for one. A female shipmate offered her car, and I thought it was pretty personal, being we were very new to the area and she wasn't a mutual friend. I hadn't met her, but the same woman had her license plates mailed to our home. She and her friend came to pick them up. He invited them in as if I weren't there. This didn't last long as I reminded everyone of my existence and escorted them to the door.

Things like this happened during the duration of our time here and I suddenly understood the hesitancy in trust of my first friend I'd met.

After giving birth to our daughter, a week later, I experienced a sense of pins sticking me in my ankles, which had swollen and I couldn't bend my knees while using the restroom or handle standing for long periods, or while brushing my teeth. The pins felt like needles inserting into my skin.

I was in our kitchen, preparing to sterilize her bottles and getting dinner ready. When I turned back to place the pot on the stove, it seemed to have moved to another location. I dropped the pot of water on the floor and couldn't find my footing. Things were whirling around to a different spot and I tried to walk out of the kitchen but couldn't and kept walking into the wall. My head pounded and hurt so badly that I thought it was going to pop off my body. I called out for help. I was rushed to the hospital, with our daughter in one hand and me over a shoulder because all my motor skills had diminished. It was the early signs of a stroke. Later, I had a grand mal seizure, several strokes, and went into a coma. It was toxicity after giving birth and I was released too soon after having my daughter. My blood pressure was 220/200. I should not have survived, according to the doctor. But I did.

When I came out of a coma, I remembered having a baby but didn't remember the gender. I remember seeing my mother, my sister, and my friend from home standing at my bedside. I remember seeing my spouse sitting off in the corner, looking as though he hadn't shaved in months. I knew something was wrong, but didn't know what. Once I was told what happened, I realized how blessed I was and just wanted to see my baby.

I had to fly back home because the ship had already departed and once I came to, my spouse had to return to duty. To say the least, this experience will always be memorable.

Once I arrived home, I learned the whole town had been praying over me over the gospel radio airwaves while I was in a coma. Gifts poured in from everywhere and sent to my mother's home. I even received a hand-carved cradle that was an heirloom to my sister's friend's family. She gave it to me but I returned it after using it because, after all, it was an heirloom. Even though I didn't have any harsh side effects from the strokes I suffered, there was some short-term memory loss and I had mini seizures that would come out of the blue. I often stared down at my daughter while having one as I would throughout her first year. I was on medication to keep it under control. They watched me closely, and I had support while caring for my daughter, and holding her in fear of possibly dropping her.

I went home after a while, with help because of my mini seizures, to get settled in before the ship returned. Things were well for a while, getting to know our daughter together. It was a lot of fun experiencing parenthood.

When it was time for the ship to leave again, I caught the train back home for six months so I could be with family. Once it was time for the ship to return, I called to say we were coming home. He told me to take my time since the ship would have to go back and forth out on the water and there would have to be watch duty a lot. (A watch system, watch schedule or watch bill is a method of **assigning regular periods of watchkeeping duty** aboard ships and some other areas of employment. A watch system allows the ship's crew to operate the ship twenty-four hours a day while also allowing individual personnel adequate time for rest and other duties.)

I thought, *Now why am I needing to take my time?* I agreed and said I would call when I was ready to come back. I lied. I changed my ticket to an earlier date and time. I needed to see what was in the way of my coming back home to someone whose been gone already for six months and was not excited to see his family upon returning.

I arrived home in a taxi, unannounced, and found out why I wasn't welcomed home with open arms. The house looked like a fraternity ward with beer bottles all over the place, along with a new roommate that had moved into our daughter's room. His shoes were in her closet, clothes all over like he'd moved in. There were condom wrappers in spots and our bedroom was in disarray like there was more than just sleeping that took place. I kicked out the roommate and went in on the actions that obviously took place.

Things didn't exactly go over well after this for a while. My trust issues shifted right in place with my friend when she didn't want to get to know me at our first meet. I focused solely on my daughter and tried to piece things together to find peace amid the storm but with a serious attitude.

I felt it in my gut that things were a mess. Already. I thought about what I agreed to and now with a baby. I felt it. I wasn't sure what our future was going to hold after witnessing straight-up disregard, disrespect, and distrust. I wasn't sure but I stayed to figure it out.

What was I going to do? The baby I prayed for daily was finally here. I'd gone through a hurricane after bringing her here and had to believe that this all was happening for a reason. Surely, I would not have been given such a blessing to face such a terrible ending. I know with everything we think the meaning of it is, is always the total opposite of what God knows it to be. So, with my attitude also came personal reasoning with myself in understanding this new life that had become mine.

Moving from duty station to duty station, it was always something that came home to me that was to be a secret but was exposed. I could see a different person in both of us. I looked toward my child and buried myself in mothering more than trying to figure out how to become a wife who needed to understand what was going on in my marriage. Maybe that was my first mistake. I don't know. Many, many months I clocked out on the wife part because I kept remembering the broken promise. It didn't even take that long to break. I was more than disappointed and more than doubtful of all, except the beautifully created and very wanted child I was given.

I'd vent to my friends so much that I grew tired for them, having to listen to me. It's hard being away from home, away from friends, away from the support and comfort of family.

Things weren't great, but what marriage is perfect? After receiving orders, we were at another duty station, and I'd gotten a job on base. Our daughter went to daycare on base and all was in place living on shore duty. I was pregnant again. I was happy and horrified because of what happened the first time. I didn't know what plans God had for me. The day I found out I was pregnant, I went into the bathroom and cried my eyes out, and had a conversation with God. Through my tears, I said, "Lord, I have to trust You and I know You didn't allow this to happen to harm me. I know You've got me." I had to trust the process even though I was terrified. My marriage was in trouble and now I was having another child. During this pregnancy, everything was going fine right down to my sixth month going into my seventh month. I was at a regular doctor's appointment, my blood pressure was elevated, and I felt those needles sticking me in my ankles.

It was happening again. My body was going through all the same symptoms. There was the fear of going through this all over again. With this pregnancy, I was at a doctor's office on an appointment and ended up in the delivery room that same day. I had to have my son that day or else it was going to be detrimental to my life and his so he had to be birthed. My body was so limp over the drugs they had put me on that I was unable to push him out. He had to be pulled out. He was premature at four pounds and so tiny but twenty-two inches long. He was perfect. White as snow with red lips and simply perfect. We were all there for him being introduced to the world and I was in love all over again like after having my daughter.

Being home with my son and daughter was everything I could ever ask for and even though my trust was out of the window, I had to put it on the back burner. My focus was on something more important. My family, so I forgave and moved forward.

However, when I forgave, it seemed one-sided. I believed this family was loved and was a proud sentiment to have especially with a son now who carried the same name. I, on the other hand, wanted to give him his own identity. Just a sidebar notation.

Love for a family can be true and irreplaceable, but when the flesh craves what it craves, Russian Roulette becomes a closer friend. I never doubted the love in the beginning and having our children, but a new world was introduced and old habits resurfaced, along with growing pride. I now have learned, however, with a new experience comes a piqued curiosity. This is where having your cake and eating to eat it, too, comes until there are no more eating contests left.

After being home from the hospital with our son, things were different. I felt unwanted and overlooked. Then there was the rumor mill at work. I'd been told about someone who was a part of my life, though I'd never met them, but was awfully close to my better half. It showed through actions at home. I was just there. When others were around, the show was put on for them to witness. We were close to home so visitors frequented our home from our hometown, which filled gaps of much-needed company. Sometimes, I'd hate to see them leave. I enjoyed the companionship and, unbeknownst to them, once I closed the door behind them, the adult interactions ceased.

Knowing in my heart things were changing, I tried to join the military for my own stability with the children. I'd just gotten past the a lotted time after giving birth to go back to work, but the military was strict with age requirements. I was told that by the time I'd gotten done with boot camp, I would be at the restricted age, so I couldn't join. I had a plan but was disappointed and had to suck it up again and focus. I had two babies who needed me outside of what I was feeling down on the inside. Had it only been me, I would've handled things differently. I knew nothing was wrong with me, yet I still questioned what was wrong with me.

Shore duty lasted for only a few years, and it was time to go to the next place.

Going to another duty station, yet again, I had hopes of a fresh start as I always did; I remained hopeful. Each place was new, so I prayed for new outlooks on things and to renew the value of family. Hmmm, not so much. It was feeling like resentment more than love. However, I rolled with things because it wasn't about me. It was about my son and daughter. However, still mentally entangled in my thinking, I wanted to keep trying since my plan to join the military hadn't panned out. I wasn't ready to fail at this, not as a mother of two. I had to try.

Unbeknownst to me, I gained most of my inner strength. This was going to be the eye-opener and truth moment that I'd have to face. I'd thought I'd dealt with the bulk of the break-in of this new life and hoped that the dust would settle and the importance of the mission and vision of what we set out to do would settle in, but it never did.

We discussed which place we would choose for the next duty station. I think to this day, what I chose amongst the choices wasn't really a mutual choice, but was mutually agreed upon. From all I'd dealt with after being allowed to choose, I felt it was some sort of payback because of what I chose. Maybe it was just my imagination running wild. Maybe.

So, here we are in a beautiful new environment and moving forward. I'm gung-ho, believing in my heart that staying was the right decision. I believed that after forgiving and even through my doubtfulness, things could still work.

At the last duty station, being shore duty meant immediate access every day and not going out to sea. I liked that better because things were hands-on and I didn't have to wonder about anything or wait to talk about things. Even though there were still some mishaps I knew of there, he was still on land. Being on land seemed to make a difference, and you have to take advantage of what you can when you can. That's what it felt like for me. I took it over anything else.

We were back at ship duty going out to sea and I can't lie, I had knots in my stomach and everything else. My nerves were on edge a little because I didn't want this and wished shore duty could have been a consistent thing. The job was a part of the package and I knew inevitably, however, we could not avoid it.

The children and I got to tour the ship, the base, and other places in the surrounding area. I had to learn my way around. I'd gotten better with knowing the different lingo that was related to the military and the requirements for assistance received when needed, etc. We met our new neighbors in housing who would later become another extended family and the children had new playmates.

Not long after we were there, it was time for the next tour out to sea and I had to get prepared. Things were all put together in our home and we had settled in with the children being comfortable and getting used to a new place. I took it for what it was, being a part of the military life. This tour, however, would be longer than usual, which was unsettling, but what could I do? The ship was a co-ed ship like before, so my mind started wandering in areas that I couldn't help but travel to. I still believed. I needed to believe.

Despite all things that happened before, moving forward continued to be my goal. I guess I downplayed those things in my mind and kept saying to myself that it could have been worse. Looking at the glass on full instead of half empty, I minimized what had caused a mountain of distrust, thinking of my children. This was a family and not a temporary lifestyle for me. It was my home and my circle, and I needed to fight and stand in the gap to keep things together. I had experienced a little bit now and had caught on to different signs, so I held onto my notes and paid attention. It didn't matter how I or anyone else felt. I was in and had no plans to be out.

CHAPTER TWO

Thunderstorms

It was the calm before the storm. A storm that I would have never predicted in a million years. A storm that made any other mishaps look like mists of rain. I got drenched and washed out in a storm that the news or anyone else could have made me believe was possible or existed.

The thing about this life is that as a military wife, you are on one side and that life, along with who you joined in it with, is on the other side of a wall with a whole other army of people. People that become their family, which you will never become related to. That family has strict rules and restrictions that you can never be a part of or reach or get through to, no matter how you place yourself in it. It will never include you, outside of the definition of your role attached, and there are a lot of times where you feel like the outsider. There is a code that is beyond your ability to break and I'd learn all too well how it protects its own.

Nights with not knowing whether work was the reason for absences or if watch on the ship was the truth went on a lot. I thought, *Wow, it didn't take long for that familiar picture to be hung on the wall.* Nights consisted of my bawling my eyes out over those missed promises to be there but weren't for different activities with the kids. Nights comprised of my getting fed up with the beginning of that storm brewing in the clouds before showing its downpour. I packed up things, balled up clothes and belongings, and threw them out of the front door on the lawn in housing, forgetting this wasn't a home bought but was owned by the military. It didn't matter to me because when you are in your emotions and hurt, you are beyond logic.

Christmas went by with my having to write both names on gifts because only one parent was present, even though both should have been home. It was always reflected, so I thought all was good in the kids' eyes because shielding things became my profession. How many know that what we think we have shielded from our kids is only a figment of our imagination? They know, they see, they hear…they're just too young and in a role where they can't say anything about it without stepping out of their places.

It was finally that time to leave for longer than the usual months required. Even though I loathed that part of that life, I was looking forward to it. At that point, it no longer mattered. Besides, the only difference between being gone out to sea and being home was not actually being home. Months into deployment, when I was the single parent at home, a lot transpired over miles and miles of water that swam its way to my doorstep once again.

Years ago, I talked to a stranger over the phone who threatened bodily harm over issues dealing with his sister. A sister I didn't know. Something happened at a port the ship docked in during its tour out. When the tour ended, and they were back home the cell phone my husband kept under a pillow, either on vibrate or silence, rang. This time, it was on vibrate. I heard it. She wasn't expecting me to answer the phone. Our conversation lasted for over an hour about how she was misled and didn't know there was still a very present and live marriage. She knew a lot of things about my life and things about my children that could have only come from one place. However, while speaking with her, she kept saying the right last name but the wrong first name so I had to ask her to describe the person she was seeking. She described him to a tee but was given a wrong first name and I corrected it. I was also hopeful she had dialed the wrong number but unfortunately, she hadn't.

She'd gotten pregnant and stated that the support was right there by her bedside while she went through a tubal pregnancy and had to have it terminated. This hurt to the bone. She told me there had been arguments because she learned of someone else besides her, in the same area. Of course, there were pleas for her forgiveness.

The woman's brother, who was livid after finding out about the deception, was ready to take a trip to confront the one who deceived his sister. I pleaded with him not to do so because my children or anyone else should not have to suffer for one person's deeds.

He stated that not only was there a soul tie connected with his sister and her children, but with his extended family members. There were barbeques and family gatherings that included the guest who portrayed himself as single and bonding with his sister's loved ones. He was told betrayal would never come as he cared for the sister deeply and there was nothing to worry about. Her brother watched closely at the word bonded and to conclude things with what he knew from the beginning angered him.

I was on the phone with a stranger, apologizing for something I had nothing to do with, but I had to put myself last and my children first.

He said to me, "You know, you sound like a real good woman, and only because of you and our conversation that I respect, I'm going to fall back. I'm known to be a man of my word, so mark my words when I say, you just saved a life today. I know his type and he is going to do it again, so you would be a fool to stick around someone who doesn't fully appreciate what he already has."

Honestly, after the conversation, I felt stupid. I was apologizing for something that tore my heart out and had to protect all the same. I was protecting what betrayed me and fought against me. I did it and still looked around the corner, hoping the man on the phone would keep his word and stay away.

Two weeks later, I received another call to my home from another woman who was only trying to find out about the number on her phone bill and to who it belonged. Before she could even start asking questions, I told her who I was and where she was calling, and confirmed my marital status. Guess who she was? The other woman to the mistress in the same state. She apologized and stated she wasn't that type of woman but also revealed that she too had conceived but had a miscarriage and again the support was there by her bedside as well. Her story was like the first: wrong name and deceit. Another blow. I thought back to that one person who said, "Girl, you are crazy if you stay a minute longer." What I thought I knew wasn't remotely close to who I felt I knew.

Confronting these issues, the world-famous, "It wasn't me" was at bay. Long days and nights of arguing became exhausting. The thoughts of my children always remained first, no matter how I felt. I needed them to understand conflicts and resolutions in a circle. This was what I felt I was doing.

After outside conversations and the cell phone on silent, which was now super-glued to the hip with his every move, I knew there were still skeletons in the closet. Even though I was the woman who had a guaranteed place in our home, I knew I wasn't the only one. I continued to turn a blind eye.

Wearing multiple masks when family visited, pretending to be a happy, picture-perfect family, was growing old but was like a broken record. I recall after a family visit; I chose to sleep in another room. I no longer wanted to sleep with the enemy. However, in the middle of the night, he coerced me to return to my rightful spot in our marital bed and it was a horrible nightmare.

When I found out from other military wives about how nice it was that the ships had docked early, I had to plaster this enormous smile and agree when I did not know or had any clue where my *disappearing act* was. When things seemed to be okay, I'd reconsider my thoughts in altering my and the children's lives, but then something else would come about that would put me right back in the same headspace.

There were late-night fake phone calls and suddenly, the job was calling to help a friend on the ship who was in a crisis. Another military wife, whose spouse was on the same ship, told me about an argument about disrespectful actions made against me in my absence and being disciplined for it. This was a couple that we spent outings with and our children played together, so we had formed a small family between us. It was embarrassing and humiliating.

I owned a mask of every color and every expression of deceit. Daily I didn't even have to pick one up. It automatically attached itself to my face to fit the theme of the day.

While living in military housing, you grow a bond with the other military wives and a group turns into a family where, like real family members, you look out for each other. We all had one thing in common: supporting our better halves in representing the United States. We'd cry together over our different mishaps and hang out together while one of their teenage daughters babysat our small ones. We formed a wives' club for support and cookouts or potlucks. We all needed that support.

As I continued to be a housewife, I applied to school. It never seemed to be the right time to go to school, for a plethora of reasons: it would be an interruption with the children, or we didn't have anyone to look after the children, and so on.

Then, our joint account was suddenly changed to an individual account. I no longer had access to any funds to support the household in his absence. At this time, we were working with one income. I attempted to have an in-home daycare to add to the household finances. However, that was short-lived because parents were taking advantage of the convenience. I called the command to report the actions of my being denied access to our account and weeks had gone by before anything was corrected and as I had on other occasions before, I was deemed as the nagging spouse.

Another military family that lived next door to us supplied money for gas, provided food out of their deep freezer and refrigerator for my family that was living and supporting the very meaning behind honor. The neighbor was a sergeant and asked if I wanted him to report it to the superiors he knew that could report what he was doing and why, to assist my family during this crisis, but I declined. It was already humiliating to have to receive help from his wife and the family. I attempted to deal with it my way. He received a slap on the hand and they reopened the account. The reasoning behind it was that I was spending too much money and later found out that my taking care of the home and the children got in the way of the fun that needed funding. How embarrassing it was to hear others speak about your loved one's ill integrity and honor toward his family. It just seemed to be a continuous part of my story of being humiliated.

A huge candy store came to mind. A kid going bonkers in an enormous candy story with a variety of choices and choosing only one piece of candy would be impossible. This was how I felt over the infidelity. How many was it going to take? After all the blown trees swaying to one side, not being able to see through the downpour, the icy feeling at the slightest touch to the skin, and just downright wet and discomforting unwanted state, this storm took out a lot more than hurt feelings. It took my will to want anything outside of peace and the children. I did not ever consider my health during the masquerade of fun. Thank you, God, for covering me.

Enough was enough. For years I'd masked all my pain. I endured the embarrassment. I protected the images. I suffered through ridicule and was made out to be the Wicked Witch of the West. I never defended myself or explained my stern and standoffish demeanor. For years in this promise for a new life, running away instead of just standing up for us, I've dealt with pretending it was going to get better. It wasn't, and it didn't. There were so many things going on I'd lost count. The dumbest thing an immature woman would think was that I must have caused it. I felt this way during these dark times in my life, trying to figure out what I must have done, but have since then learned that it wasn't me at all. I wanted things to work but had chosen me in the end because I was worth more.

So many times, I wanted to reach out to friends or family but could not vent because it was all just too much. To even say out loud what was going on put me in fear of hearing myself and admitting my truths of the blinders I was wearing.

One woman boldly confronted me, telling me she was one of the other women and she wasn't going anywhere. Of course, this stirred something in me that had been suffocated for so long. In her face, I called and relayed her message, only to be scolded as if *I* were the other woman. This confirmed more truths and woke me up. So, I snapped. I caused a physical altercation, and charges were pressed against me, and not even from the person who tried to be bold but from the person closest to me. I went to jail, got released on my own recognizance, was sentenced to see a probation officer, and had to attend anger management classes for nine months, all because of the lack of self-control issues.

I had to report to a probation officer as if I were a criminal, and report to classes as if I truly had anger management problems. Then again, it fit my description after a while because I was indeed angry. I was angry because I didn't invite any of these extra activities into my life, my home, or the sanity that I had before all of this. Yes, I was angry, so maybe the classes weren't that much of a stretch after all.

Still, having to attend anger management classes was demeaning but it taught me more than I'd expected. I met some of the bravest and strongest women in this class. Some who had done things because of betrayal that made my incidents look like a cakewalk. A few of them had to do community service and others had to do short jail time for their actions. The stories of physical abuse they received from well-respected military officials and officers, with them just protecting themselves and their children, were shocking and eye-opening. People think because there is a uniform present that it couldn't be anything outside of nobility and honor. This is far from the truth. A uniform can only give the statement the person gives. That's it.

I learned that if this was the type of person I was going to become in dealing with a life I voluntarily entered but didn't ask for the unnecessary brokenness, then I'd rather be without it. My integrity was shot during this time and my belief in what I kept trying to hold on to had diminished. I no longer believed in what it claimed to be because I lived the truth of what it was. All respect was out the window.

I sat across from the probation officer, who read me immediately, stating he could tell I had more class than my reasons for being in his office. This was one thing that woke me up, along with many other things. He saw the woman in front of him and saw things in me I hadn't owned up to yet. He confidently told me he knew he would never see me again and once my classes were over, he expected me to become great. I remember him saying, "Whatever that great thing is going to be, make sure it keeps you on the playing field of success and not defeat." I agreed and knew that once this probation was over, this life would soon be over for me as well.

Many things came to mind as I contemplated the next move. So much had happened in *this* life, I was mentally and emotionally exhausted, and disappointed in the person I had become. There were nights when I drove all over, with no destination, looking for something to confirm what I'd already knew. So, I waved the flag within. I was done.

One night as the kids slept, I was listening to a pastor who said, "You can put glue between you and another person and if they don't want to stay, there wasn't enough glue that could make them stick." He said, "Let them go." I cried until I couldn't see straight, had a massive headache, and could no longer breathe because of a snot-filled nose (just keepin' it real). I couldn't be intimate any longer because I felt nothing. I felt like just another woman with no significance. I felt hatred in my heart. I felt numb and during intimacy, I saw the faces of other people in place of mine.

It was time to remember me. It was time for me to remember that staying in an unhealthy situation for our children wasn't the right reason. The mother I'd always been toward them, owning the strength I'd always had within myself or being free to live without the mask I woke up with on my face every day, was someone I needed to be as an individual who counted. I finally chose myself.

I felt like "Sybil" when it was time to leave (for those of you who saw the movie of Sallie Fields playing multiple personalities). My feelings were all over the place as I used two weeks to leave while I was home alone once again. I talked to myself and those other people within me that I had confided in about my plans. One tried to reason with me. Another was spewing reality at me along with the scenarios I'd encountered. The other one kept reminding me of the children and my needing to figure out how to work it out. I know this sounds crazy, but if you can relate, then you know exactly what I'm talking about. There were voices in my head coming at me from all directions. In the end, I realized that no voice was more powerful than the voice of truth. God didn't intend for me to be a doormat or a convenience. I was to be a partner, wife, friend, lover, and mother who deserved respect and honor. Who, even in our trials, should have received honesty and genuine remorse.

I sold our household furniture to another military family and everything else I sold for one dollar in a garage sale. I had help from someone who was not cheering for me, but for herself, putting on the façade of a Christian. She was a little too helpful in helping me to leave, but I didn't care. I wanted out of the whole connection. She took our daughter early on to our hometown so that she could start school and I kept our son.

It was time to go. I hitched up the U-Haul to the back of the van, turned in the keys to military housing, and drove home. It was thirteen hours of driving and crying. I was full of mixed emotions, saying goodbye to the city, to the house, to the pain, and my life as a military wife. Looking in the rearview mirror at my beautiful son as he sat in his car seat playing, laughing, and singing the ABCs, I thought how nice it must be to not have any cares or worries and simply be happy. Not a care in the world besides wanting someone to love you and look after you. He made my heart smile.

Once I arrived home and he realized we had gone, I received a call, asking where I was. I confirmed my leaving, and that it was over. Then he dared to say, "I was about to stop." I'd heard that before, so I told him it wasn't necessary. I was giving him the freedom that was so obviously needed and wanted. It was time to move forward no matter what the future held; I was ready to face it.

CHAPTER THREE

Matters of the Heart

When I left, I was hurting and even though leaving was my decision and was necessary, I should have thought my next steps through thoroughly. There will always be those you lean on for support and who you want to believe and understand where you are coming from. Then there are those with whom you have a connection to that you hope will understand you out of love and not because of one-sided loyalty.

I don't know why I didn't look past my embarrassment. I should've gone to my mother's home. I now know that the reason behind this was to still try the last route at getting the attention I felt I needed by having to leave. I was new to this and have learned that no matter what's going on with anyone, loyalty comes first through some people it seems over what's right. I've learned that love can look like love but is behind a devil's advocate that's dancing over your misery.

Though I felt rejuvenated in leaving, I was still dealing with the fact that this wasn't a girlfriend-boyfriend situation but a whole marriage, which a small part of me still wanted. However, I knew it was over. I would often ask myself, *Kim, did you do all you could do to save your marriage?* Then I'd think, *Kim, you did all*

29

that you could with the cards you were dealt and because it was your choice to enter in, you saw and dealt with what took you to a certain point and made a decision. I've learned that even when we choose to do something, the outcome will show us whether it was a good or bad choice. The Word says *to not let any man put the marriage asunder*, which means to not allow anything tear it into pieces. Separation will do just that. You can't save what is out of reach. You can't pray over a situation when the parties cannot touch and agree. I also learned you can never have a successful marriage if God does not remain the solid foundation. Therefore, He says not to be unequally yoked because no matter the circumstances, if He is present the chance of a turnaround is greater.

Tastelessly, the support I was receiving was void, but I didn't see it then. When someone is eager to volunteer in assisting you to do anything and has ill intent behind it and has never supported you before in good intentions, you need to step back and take a moment. If they've shown you nothing but immature and selfish motives in making sure you understood where you stood in their eyes, take heed. Once you do this, find a truly supportive team that not only has your best interest at heart, as well as those connected to you, and execute it out of love. Back then, I don't remember hearing, "Is there anything you can do to salvage things?" or "I've been there so let me encourage you," or "Don't make hasty decisions and be sure that it's truly what you want to do." When they simply go along with things with no positive advice, please choose another outlet and another source of support. All Christians are not made equal. I learned this during my journey of growth.

Some people do things just for show, but the matters of the heart aren't in order. Their actions look like they are coming from a good place. I didn't need this from them because I had a strong support team. I was vulnerable and trusting and wasn't aware that I'd just placed myself in the enemy's camp without coverage, spewing false accusations, lies, and attempts to make a serious situation look like a nonchalant act.

During our dating phase, and our visits together, ex-girlfriends were invited to minimize my position. Drinks offered with my being deliberately overlooked, and I questioned the maturation of the person, as it was unbecoming. Childish antics were deemed as Christian efforts. Manipulating acts toward others to place doubt because of selfishness. I'd vowed that it would never happen to my children, but it did. God always has precedence over what's not right. I never needed the approval from the beginning, but my heart has always been one to give the benefit of the doubt before I react. I should have pounced instead of giving the benefit. It's okay. I'm better off without the attachments, but at the time all I wanted was a great relationship and decency in respect.

Now I know it was only plain unwise. While I was depressed, unhappy, and misplaced in my thoughts and trying to mother our children, it was an eerie thing to have the enemy smiling right in my face, looking me straight in the eye, and have no love for me or my wellbeing. I didn't care about that because there were people who loved me and eventually my good senses kicked in and I removed myself from the drama and went where I knew I belonged.

Simply trying to make sense of the chaos I was in while being talked about behind my back, despite what the enemy tried, I persevered through eventually. Like a dog carrying a bone, the same people who were told these things were the same ones who saw the true person who stood before them, speaking ill of me and would make me aware of the words spoken. I grew up believing in right being right no matter who you are or your connections.

Truth always prevails. Even if at one point I'd been told that what I experienced was close to the same thing that some had gone through while affiliated with the military and had to pack up with kids and leave. Thinking of this I thought that maybe amnesia got the best of them or the stories were all a lie just for conversation purposes by revealing their pasts of dealing with the same type of situation as I was currently dealing with at the time. Real sincerity in a person shows throughout a lifetime and it has been a lesson learned for me. I was right where I belonged in my time of need and that was with my family.

Trying to fight to protect my truth and prove it was the hardest thing to do because I cared about what others thought and it seemed that just telling the truth wasn't making it easy. For years I kept all of it pinned up and mirrored to fit a certain life. No more. My truth reflected who I was and what I wanted and hoped my children would grasp hold of in their adulthood. Even if the whole truth and nothing but the truth didn't set you free all the time. Still, truth abounded in the end.

My story isn't any different from anyone else's who is dealing or have dealt with grief, pain, or misguided truths protecting others in their wrongdoing. Especially if some aren't fond of you anyway, the accused could never do any wrong. But God sees and He knows. This is what I've had to hold onto through the duration of my life and have been covered with it. A warrior always goes by timing and patience towards victory.

This is to empower you to still speak and stand by your truths even if it looks like you're losing a battle that seems too big to win. Stand behind facts and history of connections that weren't so polite and believe in what it shows you.

Sometimes because the ones who are raising the most hell have a huge crowd behind them it makes you feel defeated and they are allowed latitude because of what the surfaces reveal. It looks like they must be in the right regarding what's going on if they say it then it must be gold. The more you stream what's really going on (the truth) the more you seem to be the one who's the aggressor. When we know that a situation isn't right or fair, we tend to become overly emotional while shouting out truths but it's not taken this way. The only thing that is witnessed is the outbursts and demeanor of the person in pain. Again, I know this all too well.

After so long, I started to question myself as to what the truth really was and was it as bad as the shouts that were being bought forth. It was. I began to think that no matter what I said I was going to be the bad person or the one who had all the issues. How I got to this place I will never know. How it got to the point where being unmarried became a worse nightmare than the regular dream of being married was beyond me. My life was changed more so afterward than during and I would have never imagined the length of time it had attempted to run my life.

I've moved my entire being to cope with a lot of broken issues. I had shut down and even at times said, "Okay, you win," to the enemy just so he would stay away and out of my life. I remember stating various times how I forgave and that forgiving was how life could move forward and parenting could go smoother. It felt sometimes that I was going crazy all because of one uniform speaking so many volumes and yelled the total opposite of all truths and I couldn't prove it. I was the silent and invisible person in a lot of ways even though I was screaming truths at the top of my lungs. When there are children involved it is never easy to tackle stability in the middle of chaos. You try but even if you move from state to state searching for a breath of fresh air, the smog and smoke follow you and the brokenness continues. The only way I was going to mend what was broken was to face all the shattered pieces head-on no matter how many times I got cut.

How do you say the words love and hate in the same sentence and it makes sense to you? I was deflecting blame on the signs that floated in front of me from the beginning but had already stepped into it so I used this to justify staying. Deflecting blame on others over my hurt after all was settled because I tried to state the truth a long time ago but no one listened. So, I began to breathe with every new conversation I had with the Father. I began to see clarity in my mistakes and shortcomings and was okay with not being okay. I was okay with all that had happened up to this point because I had no choice. I'd made the move and now it was time to do what I had to do.

People took my pain and twisted it in a sickening way to fit and protect the wrongdoings of others. I was told so many times about conversations had in attempts to make the main one who caused everything to look like the victim. So sad it was to not only feel like a failure having to come back home but sadder to have to be informed consistently of things being said to protect the outlook of what was in the wrong. I not only felt like a failure, I felt like what other women think when they want to be a replacement in a relationship like I'd done all the things that would have caused me to have to move back home separated and soon to be unmarried.

I was so angry and mean towards so many people who loved me and for that, I'll always pray that I am forgiven. I was angry because I was back home, I was angry because I'd left, I was angry because if things would have been done differently from the beginning I would not have gotten to this point in the first place, I was angry that I'd chosen this life without counsel, I was angry that I was too young from the start to jump and leap like I had all of the answers in life like I knew what was best for me in making such a huge decision over my life. I was angry that I didn't take full advantage of going off with my mouth with the power I knew I had to cut through a person's heart with my words, I was angry at myself for maintaining my composure and angry because angry felt like the appropriate emotion to be.

There isn't any explanation as to how it feels when knowing your marriage is ending. It doesn't matter what caused it; it was about to be over. In all the pain there was still love inside that was ending. Although I'd chosen to end things, it didn't make things lighter or me the bigger person to call it a truce. It didn't make me better for taking the first step at this decision. It's a horrific situation to be in. It is indeed like a death because even when you don't understand the spiritual side of becoming one, automatically it feels like a part of your body is dead and wounded.

A part of me wished that I could rewind things to see if there was something that I could have done differently to change the outlook of the parties involved in not having self-control. I was ashamed that I chose not to be a trooper and stay to see it through. Mortified at the least was how I felt coming back home, having to look into my children's faces, wondering what they were thinking. If they'd had any questions or wishing they would ask so, at least, I would know where their minds were. They were young so I didn't know if they even had the questions to form toward what was going on. They simply wanted things to continue to be happy around them and for their parents to take care of them.

God, so much was going on in my mind at this point and I was always wondering what my family was thinking about my having to come home. What others thought was so important to me because I hadn't grown into myself and my self-worth. Too scared to ask what others thought and others were too scared to ask questions.

Walking away from a marriage is not as easy as one, two, three, nor is it "Hear me roar and respect my huge egotistic move to leave." Those who make it seem as though it is have not only lied to others but themselves as well.

This hurt. This was complicated and scary. This was being exposed and no longer secure in a definite thing. This was the difference between being attached and unattached and having to be a part of the single world once again. This was not a party. It was nightmares and nightmares even though I chose to wake up and walk away.

The heart is stronger than any other organ we possess. Out of it flows the character of a man. All I know is during all of the back-and-forth emotions, hesitancy with the decision making, and uncertainty of the outcome of things, I still knew that my chosen plan was the right one. I just needed to get through the red tape of the journey it took to be okay with my choices.

Love is anything but what it is meant to be. Until we teach those how to love along the lines of respect, standards, and expectations knowing what we have become a part of will always cause us to be blindsided from not placing honesty upfront.

We can't take fault when another person can't handle the weight of our value that comes in the form of strength and a rightful place of self-worth. Just because it's not valued doesn't mean that it isn't valuable. We teach love through how we love ourselves. It is a learned thing to love within because we were born into sin and going by the ways according to all laws of the land and mimicking the need to be approved of first before loving self.

Yeah, I was back home now. I had to strategically plan my life along with my children's. So, it had come time for me to place all the whining, the victim mentality, and the anger behind me and put on my big girl underwear and move forward. I had not a clue as to where to start or who to call but I was about to learn. Learn things that I would have never known.

I learned that false love comes in all sorts of packages. All you can do in growth is pray over it because false love can't love if it doesn't exist within. It was time to grow up and face my decision and forward march.

CHAPTER FOUR

Knowledge of Military Versus Civilian Divorces

If you are contemplating divorcing a spouse who is in the
military, *please* do your homework. *I can't stress this enough!* Going
through your circumstances in getting what you need to execute
your goals through military versus civilian will impact every order,
decision, and/or the aftermath you will face. It could end up being
for your good or for your bad, all based on the knowledge that you
have on the dos and don'ts in this type of situation. Don't rely on
anyone else to tell you everything. *Research!* Just as you are reading
my experience and story, it is indeed *my* experience and story. Your
story may be similar but not a mirror to mine. There are different
avenues we have to take that will fit our needs. Please research.

A couple of months had gone by since I'd left. I was still
trying to figure out where I was to go from here. The loss of my
marriage devasated me, even though I'd initiated it. I was not
mentally prepared or knew where to start. However, it was time to
face the music and do what I needed to do. I was afraid. I had two
babies who depended on me to nurture and care for them. The
children were used to him not being around, and they were very
young. Although I had my babies, I was mentally, emotionally,
and physically flying solo. A friend said, "Girl, forget it and move

on. Women have been doing this for years, raising their children without deadbeat fathers and you can do it, too." So, my first step was to relocate to family, where I should have in the beginning.

While I heard her but I didn't believe it was the appropriate definition for my circumstances. I believed it was simply the phase of finding this new life that took over morals and values that led to chaos. That chaos would eventually affect my children, who didn't choose to partake in any of this. I had gone through so much that I wasn't willing to let things be without strategically concluding the outcome of all enjoyment. When you play, you get dirty. If you like being dirty, when it's time to be scrubbed down, you must deal with it.

The hatred and heartless acts toward not only me but to my family, and the lies made it worth every step I had to make. I pondered on the thoughts of double lives had while away from home that was bought to my attention, name changing and causing distraught throughout other households. My having to talk someone out of coming to do bodily harm for the sake of my family and in all of this, lessons still hadn't been learned over the value in the blessing that was had. It was worth it to me, even if no one else understood.

So, my mother had a friend who was an attorney whom we retained to assist me in obtaining support for the children. Income was an issue as I had walked away from my marriage and not working. It was spread throughout my family and friends that I never wanted to work or go to school, and I only wanted to stay at home with the kids, which couldn't have been further from the truth. Nothing I wanted to do was a good fit into the life and career I had chosen. Once, during a phone conversation, my mother asked me, "Why is it that every time you get accepted to school to better yourself or a great opportunity comes along, it's never the right time?" There was never a solid answer as I was big on submission even though I was making most of the decisions due to this military life and separation. I felt I was doing the right thing by my marriage and our family. At any rate, I needed to figure out how I was going to take care of attorney fees, etc. My mother *(bless her heart)* extended all she could to keep my issues from drowning because of finances.

The legal process was new, and I was at a loss; I didn't know what to expect, do, or say. I truly wasn't aware of all of my rights as a military spouse facing a divorce. I knew nothing about the many options I had that I could've given my attorneys nor did I know anyone who'd gone through this as a military spouse to guide me in the directions that would assist me. (The attorney fees were steep and I had gone through a few attorneys, and one removed themselves because I couldn't afford their fees.) I knew a lot of spouses going through this ordeal but none who took the steps to leave. Therefore, I'm writing this to help, inform, relate, and heal by letting it out and letting it all go. Not only is this helpful for military-affiliated women who must deal with divorce, but it is also an encouragement for civilian women who may go through the same. Again, *do your research*.

Sidebar: The information I'm about to share is based on my being an ex-military wife and what I've learned through the process. So, for civilian spouses who might be dealing with a similar, unfortunate situation, please excuse me a bit while I give the information below.

The military has unique legal assistance that helps with complex things that could lead you to make better decisions and have fairer outcomes. Dealing without military informative knowledge will not help you get the proper representation and the maximum conclusion in all your entitlements. The military legal department will not represent you in court as their legal department is only there to inform you of all of your rights and all you are entitled to depending on the years of marriage while that person is active duty. They consider divorce as a private civil matter that needs to be addressed by civilian courts, which has given me a clearer picture of the saying, yet again, "Your family doesn't come in your seabag."

If you are a military member, there are choices you are told you have as far as getting a divorce. It's called SCRA: Soldiers and Sailors Civil Relief Act which allows the service member to request a "stay" (that is, to delay the proceedings), a divorce, or other claims (such as spousal support, custody, child support, property division, and military division) if their duties prevent them from participating in or responding to the court action. The three choices a military service member trying to initiate the divorce are: 1) The state where the spouse filing resides, 2) The state where the military member is stationed, or 3) The state where the military member claims residency.

They asked me about alimony and had no knowledge of it then, but I know now. A spouse's military service time will not determine whether you are entitled to alimony in your divorce. Federal military laws do not set guidelines on alimony awards and veterans can't be ordered to pay more than fifty percent of his or her income toward support. Also, just like a civilian spouse, the military spouse is held responsible for paying spousal support. Being in the military is no reason for the nonpayment of spousal support.

Benefits as far as access to military bases, commissary, and exchange privileges after divorces are final and are only given to those who have been married for twenty years or more. This also applies to continuing to keep your military identification and military insurance for inpatient and outpatient care at a military treatment facility. It will not apply if you have been married less than twenty years. The Uniformed Services Former Spouses' Protection Act exempts VA disability payments from division upon divorce. It is not an asset that can be divided after divorce as marital or community property. The funny thing about this is that once you come to the end of the road, getting on the military base means nothing and isn't worth fighting for. This was me. Learning this bit of information was pertinent, but not crucial.

I did not know the first thing to tell my attorneys as to military spouse's rights when going through this. All I knew was that his income far more exceeded mine when we needed to figure out child support. I knew about the military pay Leave and Earnings Statement which was something I had to explain and get a copy.

Because "I didn't do my homework," I couldn't tell my attorney that when a person was active duty, the child support could have been based on their Base Pay, BAH *(Basic Allowance for Housing)*, BAS *(Basic Allowance for Subsistence)* and any other special pays of the service member. In my case, wages was still being collected and earned through BAH for having dependents at home and it was never reported that we were no longer in the home and had the documentation to prove it. However, because I didn't know that it was very relevant information that could've made a difference, I didn't use it.

Dealing with the anxiety of whether you will receive child support or other support can be hectic. I need you to know that it is important to retrieve this information from your affiliated branch because each branch of service offers different levels of assistance in these matters. It is also important to be aware of all you are entitled to before the court order is placed because this overrides any guidelines the military has in place, so you want to make sure you are more than knowledgeable on everything.

In the event of nonsupport, the spouse requesting support should start with the service member's commander. If a resolution is not happening at that level, then contact the local JAG office, then possibly the inspector general. Support provided outside of a court order cannot be made through garnishment. It is up to the service member to set up an a lotment or provide the support directly. The command can, however, encourage the service member to provide such support and use remedies such as officer FITREPs, enlisted evals, and non-judicial and judicial punishments as appropriate. Also, DFAS can recoup BAH that has been paid to the service member and has not been appropriately used for the support of the family. It doesn't happen often, but it is possible. This is the part that I didn't know and could have used to my benefit.

Air Force guidelines can be found at: **Air Force Instruction 36-2906, Personal Financial Responsibility**, Army guidelines can be found at: **Army Regulation 608-99, Family Support, Child Custody and Paternity**, Coast Guard guidelines can be found at: Coast Guard regulations regarding family support can be found in **Commandant Notice 1000, Chapter 8.M, Support of Dependents**, The Marine Corps explains the support it recommends in the **Marine Corps Manual for Legal Administration,** Chapter 15, Financial Support of Family Members and the Navy guidelines for family support can be found in the **MILPERSMAN Section 1754-030, Support of Family Members**

One thing is for sure: the military requires the service member to provide adequate support for children regardless of an order or not. I also didn't report the changes in pay that were given based on Deployments, Hazardous Pays, Base Transfers, and other factors like Special Duty Assignment, Flight Deck pay, etc., because I didn't know the variations it played in income increases.

For those who are suffering from PTSD (Post Traumatic Stress Disorder) and have been accused of being an unfit parent by the other spouse, there are resources to help you. The National Institute of Mental Health breaks it down into two categories: a chronic ongoing condition or an acute short-term condition. To even be diagnosed as such, symptoms must last more than a month and have to be severe enough to interfere with relationships or work. Unfortunately, a bitter spouse wanting to hurt the other could try to use this and because the legal system really doesn't understand the truth behind this disorder, they fall for whatever is accused. The only thing the naked eye (court systems) knows is that it is trauma from past situations that could cause a person to act irrationally, and this is only from hearsay through news and media. They automatically relate it to military life.

So, if one were in the military and diagnosed with this, it wouldn't matter if their symptoms are acute or chronic. It is used in a custody case the first time the accused loses their composure from being gained up on by the co-parent. The best attorney to have in this case is a family law attorney who understands the unique struggles and can ensure you are well represented.

It's crazy to me that on one hand, it's almost like punishing the traumatized military member who fought for the United States, and on the other hand, courts can't see behind the schemes of the co-parent who's taking advantage of what is a blow to the outcome of serving.

For those who need healing through this or are dealing with such trials through courts, you must take the steps that will help you prove yourselves. For veterans, **1-877-WAR-VETS** is a confidential call center that works around the clock to help combat veterans and their families. There are also Veteran Centers set up to help transition members of the military into civilian life. For civilians, there are treatment centers, such as **Bridge to Recovery, Magnolia Creek and Recovery Ranch** dedicated to helping individuals suffering from PTSD.

Staying informed is key. I learned this the hard way. I was so into my feelings about being hurt and in pain, I allowed my emotions to decide and not hardcore facts in my options. So, I'm taking this opportunity to give what I didn't give to myself. It is horrible for the co-parent to use what wasn't taken on voluntarily against the very person who had a hand in giving life to the most precious gift as children. The condition should never be a reason to lose a child, but the simple fact that seeking help from it shows the courts that you are putting the children first. You would do this by making yourselves well. *It does not make you unfit.* If anything, it sets an example to children that when there are issues beyond our control, we have to seek help.

I could not speak on the legalities regarding the entitlements I was to receive, even though I qualified through the legal number of years of active-duty services given to receive certain things. A lot of missed information went over my head because I did not do my homework. Please be sure, before making such a life-changing decision to get a divorce or even separation, to research the smallest of clauses that could make or break your outcome.

Sometimes, I went to court solo with the other party being present telephonically with being active in the military and couldn't physically appear. We went back and forth because the support was being resisted. Because I didn't have all the above knowledge I mentioned, the civilian courts simply went by their state child support guidelines. Which meant both of our take-home incomes, and the total of children we had together, and wages were garnished.

Emotions were flying all over the place because I now must force an order that should not have been forced at all. I felt like even though I'd finally left, I was losing because my children were taking a hit, too.

Most military members hide behind the uniform and this would be something I'd experienced throughout the hell I was to go through for years to come behind this event.

I was angry at the world, even though the world had done nothing to me. I was numb, walking out of the courthouse, with ill feelings of not knowing how to feel. There was a sense of relief over not having to depend on family and friends to help until I got on my feet, but a sense of guilt was present, too. It's hard to be angry and ask for help at the same time from those you are shutting out. I remember blocking out those who repeatedly said, "It's going to be okay" and remember being against any advice or consolation given and feeling like I was the one who'd messed up and that no matter what I'd say in my defense it didn't appear it would ever be okay.

Putting my life (or failed marriage) on blast was not in the cards for me. I've always been private regarding my personal space. How was it I felt bad? I don't know, but I did. I was now in the wind, so to speak, having to find my way and with children who didn't know the adult roles that needed to be executed. They were and remain my strength in everything.

You don't plan on one of the biggest steps you've made in your life to come to this type of grief. You don't expect divorce court to become a part of your union. Facing a judge on any level is already nerve-wracking because whatever fate you are going to have is at his or her mercy. You cannot predict what a particular judge will recommend or if they will either have compassion or no compassion for you. Standing in front of them, wishing that they knew all the true details of what you really need from them, is so hard because you can't sit with them alone and pour out the whole truth and nothing but the truth. It all lies within the words of the attorneys, who can only go by what you tell them, and even then, you don't have your whole life or the time to give it to them straight. It must be brief and straight to the point, but a lot of points weren't shown because of the time and money that's required. You try to remember those key things and despite that, you miss something.

We say we don't care about what others think because they don't and won't know what we've been through, but that's a lie. At least when you don't know who you are in Christ. I knew Him, prayed out to Him, leaned on Him, looked at my babies and saw Him but I didn't fully focus on Him or trust that He was the head in my situation. So, I cared about what others thought about my coming back home broken, feeling if I could turn back time, I would have never gotten married. My marriage broke into pieces and the fact that the lies talked about me...well, they must have been true because all they saw was an angry me. I was the one returning home feeling as though I obviously wasn't good enough to have those things done to me in the first place.

I was now back in the civilian world, where no one understood military life or divorce laws or rules. I, too, was at a loss as to what to fight against as far as my rights. How could I know about something I never planned to go through? It was like the blind leading the blind.

Going to court for child support was just the beginning of what I would face. Seeing the walls of justice and staring at a judge, deciding my life's fate. I wouldn't have imagined my own story being about me and not a *Lifetime* Movie. A movie it wasn't, but disbelief, intimidation, and humiliation it was.

Trying to figure out my next step and where my situation was headed always seemed at bay. Thank God for my pain, my struggles, my confusion, my lessons, and my breakthroughs. I thank Him for it all because *I am still here.*

Understanding all that needs to be known about your situation and plans is pertinent. Maybe had I known every step I needed to take during the court proceedings, I could have cut my court appearances shorter. Maybe if I had known my options over what to fight against and straightforward inconsistencies made on the other party's part, I could have saved myself from pain I didn't have to endure.

In the end, I thought the bitterness would subside after the initial bout of court sessions over child support. Foreseeing future friendships with the courts was way off my calendar of appointments. I saw firsthand what anger, regret, bitterness, jealousy, and what was too late to turn around did to a man. It caused a volcanic explosion for years to come. Years that made me sick, depressed, troubled, discouraged, dispirited, gloomful, and suicidal. It made me doubtful of my choice to leave, thinking that compared to all I'd experienced, it would have been better to have never left, and I went through loads of distressing moments. For years, these moments of ill-gotten emotions bid behind a smile and mask because I still had to live and survive through it all alone. Even though people were walking, talking, encouraging, and laughing around me, I was the one who opened each subpoena received back-to-back, alone. But I'm still here. I survived. Looking back on those days, sometimes it was awfully hard to fathom that I was the one in that horror of a nightmare. Still, I crawled, cried, hated, felt waves and stirring in my stomach with every court date, skin flushed, sweat spells, and screams out to God as to when it was all going to end and I still made it out.

See, I can honestly say that just because we go through trenches of darkness doesn't define the outcome and there is, indeed, a light at the end of the tunnel. It's God and Him alone that got me through, even when I wasn't asking Him to. He did. Starting over was scary, but it was worth the journey.

CHAPTER FIVE

Remembering and Moving Forward

Flashbacks continued to come and go often over my marriage and things that were experienced while going through my divorce. When depression set in, I was raising our beautiful children with the help of everyone. I often replayed all the different females, going to jail, going to anger management classes, protecting images, and taking judgments undeserving from others. Flashbacks of scenes of infidelities that went on along with shipmates temporarily moving in while I was away, abandoning not only me but our children by closing accounts and other things that it would take far past the length of this book to name. The list continued to go on and on in my head. I would look at our babies, thinking, *How could I be the villain in the end?*

I was told I had control issues and had issues with finances. Managing my finances was a challenge because for years it was only me and all I'd done for me was for me alone and the effects of my spending only affected me. So, this principle stuck with me for a while. The thing that we become accustomed to and being for years takes just that length of time to undo or change. It was embarrassing to me. It was what it was and I owned it. I asked for help as a couple and if we could talk about it and figure out a budget. I was told that I should already know. The ask for help fell on deaf ears. I presented a solution to fix a problem that ended up feeling like a mistake and the fact that it may just work, along with making it seem like we were working together as a married couple, came too easy. Possibly it could cause some to act right or guilty about extracurricular activities. I wanted to learn how to manage finances better. Later, I did it without help. I did it by stepping back and taking myself out of the equation. It was no longer me in my circle.

He said I was controlling, which I find humorous because I would make sense out of things that weren't accepted. After all, the bad behavior was more fun to be in. The strength and confidence I had was a hindrance to an ego. This seemed to be my only fault.

Starting over to rebuild yourself with children isn't easy, but doable. Having the weight of life on your shoulder, which can seem heavy, makes it look as if the leeway is far away. It's not, we just have to trust the process. I needed to find myself again, and this wasn't a simple task as I'd become every person in one but "me." Leaving was what I wanted and needed to do, but was afraid to do many times over as I'd contemplated. I didn't want our children to grow up without both parents in the same household. I feared that once they knew I was the one who left that they would blame and that God would be mad at me for making such a huge decision. It wasn't easy, but for me, it was necessary.

So, attempting to begin again after walking away from many years of being attached was as devastating as leaving. Time had nothing to do with grieving over walking away. Attachments are attachments no matter what form they come in and detaching from a soul tie just isn't that easy.

I was immune to a certain way of living, whether it was positive or negative. Forget about the ones who say, "Girl, if that were me, I'd,"blah, blah. Those are the ones you don't want to listen to because truth is, if it were them going through the same thing, they would decide either the same way, worse or allow the chips to fall as they may and live with it because starting over would be too much of a challenge. You don't know what you would do until faced with a harsh reality where you are losing ground and trying to gain it back. No one is exempt from heartbreak and no one is exempt from not knowing how to handle it.

That safety net of feeling secure, investing life, nobility in really honoring your title, and not having it any longer to just being single can cause a shakeup in anyone. Living life with purpose and commitments means something. It meant something to me and despite the two things used to demean me, I lived up to the standards, requirements, and vows until I was tired of living them. Letting go was one thing, but holding on was suicide by default.

Living the life of a military wife and accepting the separation between each other for months became a new normal. The separation becomes a family member. You can only fix issues in increments when the issues get real and their time home is limited because you know they need to leave again to go out to sea. You aren't granted time to fix what they don't see is broken. It's out of your control because, well, it's his job and you're no match for trumping the career because, as the popular saying goes again, "Your family don't come in your sea bag."

Sometimes it was time for sea duty and talking over the phone couldn't fix what needed to be fixed face to face. Many times, I envisioned myself swimming across the sea to the ship just to finish a conversation that was abruptly interrupted by being hung up on, knowing that the connections were already hard to maintain and or connections being reached between water and land. Only having the choice of waiting until the decision to call again came about. You start feeling like a burden more than a wife. Choosing to keep forgiving and allowing others to think it was always you who was causing so much unhappiness and stress. I remember most people looking upon us as the ideal couple and remember one person who was so upset at the break-up tearing up over it. I stated to them that what was seen on the outside was the makeup I applied and performed to protect the downpour that happened on the inside.

This is not the life that I had envisioned, even though I understood what the job entailed. How can you maintain a vision when the pieces that were included of what you were promised and hoped for are scattered across the water on a ship? Pieces that are anchored in different parts of the world and at someone else's house whose name wasn't on a lease, contracts, insurances, or marriage certificate?

I convinced myself that the promise made in the beginning of agreeing to this life would resurface; the promise that we would always be okay and remain a strong unit. I taught myself that I was a wife, not a girlfriend, so I needed to learn how to stick in there because the outside was out there, and I was on the inside. I kept telling myself that I had the upper hand. I didn't though. The world had it and the new outlook of life that was handed to an individual had changed everything.

All the playing I did with my thoughts ended up yelling at me and the tears my eyes had gotten used to was overflowing with the swelling result of exhaustion. I knew that with what this career entailed, also entailed commitment, accountability, integrity, courage, and honor. I knew that the security I was to appreciate wasn't cradling my worth or mental stability. How could you give to a nation what seemed to be a disability towards giving to your own family?

Anyway, I faced living a whole new life with children and a deposit of child support that was good for supplying financial needs. It did nothing for emotional needs, unanswered questions of who, what, when, and why, mixed feelings that I had no control over at that moment, bitterness, strife in my heart, and no husband.

I didn't know which part to connect to because my brokenness didn't know which part was strong enough to hold the rest of me up. It's just a mess and in all the opinions on what you should or could do, no one can ever speak to the functioning that's happening on the inside. Again, seeing people laughing and seemingly stress-free as though the world was their oyster, so full of life and happiness and wanting so badly to get to that point but it wasn't happening fast enough, and wanting to feel "normal" seemed like my everyday challenge. Normal like not feeling alienated from happiness.

Yes, it may appear I was playing victim since I was the one who left. I was a victim. A victim of believing in my fairytale and having the nerve to want to see that thing through with my white picket fence. A victim honoring a one-sided marriage until I called it out and had done what I never wanted to do. I was a victim holding confidence in what God hadn't joined together but because we joined it, neither one of us knew enough to stand on that type of Word. We had conformed to our own way. So yes, I was victimized because I wanted what all women wanted. I wanted to live out the duration of my fairytale that was supposed to remain my reality. It instead became my dysfunctional nightmare.

But I learned, too, that being a victim can either allow you to see the conqueror in yourself or the defeated. It will show you who you are, someone you didn't even know existed in your victimization. I was a warrior in the making.

I had extremely low self-esteem then, very insecure and vulnerable. I took being a mother as serious as breathing and I needed to get on my feet, suck it up and hang up my sulking cloth. I knew it was time to step into faith and believe in myself once again, like before marriage, with all the confidence I held. Now it was going to be with two beautiful angels to care for. I had to get ready.

I loved moving to different places, which was something I'd done before marriage. I never lived the predictable or common way everyone thought things should go. Being affiliated with the military and moving to different parts of the world suited me just fine. Where to start was the question.

I sat at the computer and began my search. I was asked why I didn't want to stay home where support would be with having the children, my answer was needing to have a fresh start at life without so many voices and opinions of how the guidelines should go according to them. Moving to a different place was needed so I could reconnect with my children from my being so gone mentally. I never wavered from motherhood with them. However, my mental state while doing it wasn't fair to them because I was falling apart and like a puzzle, there were pieces thrown in places that you had to reach far to grab. I wanted them to know that we were going to be okay, even though they didn't understand the inside scoop of what was going on. Loving on them was at the forefront of my priorities, and I needed them to know that I loved them no matter the situation. The healing process became important to me as I needed to think and answer questions that had yet to form.

I hadn't realized that with the time that had passed, I was using all sorts of reasons why I couldn't move past my anger and feelings at failing at what I thought was my job to conquer.

During my reasoning, God was nurturing me and whispering things to me I couldn't hear for the loudness of my own voice. The strength He was going to pour into me with my situation would be enough even through oncoming traffic and storms. Even though I couldn't hear Him at the time, He showed me I wasn't alone. He also showed me I could start to let go. I was moving forward and it was okay.

I'd found a place that was affordable, climatically warm, and beautiful. Was I ready to take this leap? I wasn't sure, but I'd jumped and took that drive to our unknown. I was always up for a challenge and competed against myself all the time, so it was going to be or not to be. I wouldn't have known without taking the leap.

Now to plan. I told my mother what my plans were and, of course, she questioned a lot of things as to the distance between it and our hometown, but was okay that I wouldn't completely be by myself with no family around. I had family within a few hours from where I'd chosen, so it was okay. I know my situation concerned her. She wanted me to stay close to her, but I needed to stand on my own and not have the fallback available. I didn't want to depend on anyone to carry me if I fell. I wanted to stretch through the okay and not so okay times as a woman, parent, and fighter. My goal was to give it my all and to put my boxing gloves on. I was facing my new life and challenges. Whether I won or loss would be a different story.

We said our goodbyes, packed up the vehicle (Praise God for His traveling mercies because the vehicle I was forced to keep had seen its days of the highway going from state to state and she still kicked like a brand-new vehicle. But God!), loaded it up with snacks, Capri Suns, blankets, toys and all the necessities needed for long travel with children. I made it into an adventure with just the three of us. It was as if this was a long-extended vacation (which it was; it was a nineteen-hour drive) to a destination none of us were certain of but headed towards.

We stopped plenty of times during our trip to restroom breaks, eating, or just sightseeing. In my own space, unbeknownst to my children, I'd stare at them while they were eating or playing with each other and would feel so thankful to God that He chose little ole me to oversee these two. They were simply beautiful and despite the absences, when it was present, we as a team raised them okay together. I won't take that away from him. Somewhere, it began to be just me and, in the absence, I continued and added to the list because I wanted wisdom, truths, not being bias in things but to analyze what's in front of them and clarity to be deposited in them. They both started talking at a very early stage as I or anyone around them didn't speak the baby language to them (at my request) but whole words and sentences. They both learned things very quickly and always asked such deep questions and made profound statements that our communication needed little help.

We sang songs, played the license plate game, trying to figure out the definition of what the letters and numbers meant, and talked about where we were going. I knew questions would come eventually about their dad and I was ready to answer on the level that they would understand. Our son was five years younger than our daughter but was so mature for his age that it wasn't hard to explain things to him. Our daughter was born with a genius way of thinking. From toddler on, she never missed a beat in understanding things and she'd always look as though she was thinking everything through to the end before deciding to do or say a certain thing. They were used to us leaving ahead to prepare and get situated when it was time to relocate from one duty station to the next. So, when the first question came up from our daughter, asking if their father coming later wasn't a shock.

A huge gulp followed by a hard swallow and a quick prayer for help in talking about it before I spoke. One thing I stood firm on was not to lie to my children. I told them the truth and explained it to them the way I felt they would understand it. Kids aren't dumb by far and my children pay attention to everything, just as all kids do. Even when we think they are in the next room and can't hear or when they are preoccupied with television or playing with games or toys, they hear and are tuned in to everything else around them.

While at home at my mother's, I know they heard all the comments, saw me crying, and heard harsh things being said about my situation. We know that it's not good for children to hear these types of opinions and angered reactions to pain. It's difficult to get into the practice of an instant etiquette way of withholding your emotions until the appropriate time because all you know is the "right now" feelings and your "right now" expressions to those feelings. So, I know that in the atmosphere of things they knew something was off and not normal, but the details were not known to them and I was determined to make the understanding as harmless and nurturing as I possibly could.

I answered her question by telling them that this trip was different. It wasn't how it used to be where we were going to set things up before everyone came back together and that it was going to be just us this time. They wanted to know where their dad was going to be and I told them he was going to still be out on the water and doing his job and that we needed to take care of some adult things between us and it was going to take some time to do. I told them that while we were taking this time, I was finding us a home of our own to live in with just the three of us and that they would go to a new school and meet new friends. I knew that part would not be anything hard for them to understand because moving was what we did, and going to a different school was what our daughter was used to and now our son would be going, too.

My mission was to make this transition with as much ease as possible. Thank God my answers were enough for the moment and the questions stopped for now. Whew. I wondered, however, if the answers I gave them were satisfactory, and did it sit well with them to not feel any kind of way out of sorts. I didn't want them to feel uncomfortable or feel like they were a part of the problem at all.

When it was time to stop and sleep for the night, we checked into a hotel and I made it into our own pajama party and ordered pizza as we watched movies and talked about them when they were over, or different things that, thank God, had nothing to do with what was going on. We talked about the possible way the schools would be or the people we'd meet and the church we'd attend. When I look back on that time, I remember laying in the middle of my children in the single-bed hotel room with tears rolling down my face. Looking up at the ceiling, then at them, wondering exactly how starting over was going to be and would I be successful at it. The one thing I was confident about was being a mother, a friend, a lover of the heart, a trustworthy person and I thought being a wife would work itself out even with the infidelity. I thought we would just work things out and as a family we'd be able to move forward.

I had to believe that I'd made the right decision to leave. I wasn't sure but what I did, I did. Hearing him say "I was about to stop" rang in my ears and the voices of the two women who'd gotten pregnant were ringing in my ears. The man's voice over the phone that told me how stupid I would be if I'd stayed continued to repeat to me like a scratched record. For a while, I repeated these steps of thoughts in my head and not in any order. I finally acted on what was whirling around from a small circle of sand turning into a huge tornado, and it suddenly gave me strength. It gave me new confidence in the destination I'd chosen for the children and myself. It gave me faith, even in my uncertainty. I went to sleep and got some rest for the remainder of our journey.

I'd researched, found a house and saw multiple pictures of it online, and paid to stay there before we arrived. Yes, it was a risk, but I could decorate a box and make it look like a mansion, so I took the leap of faith. Upon arriving, it wasn't a disappointment at all and was quite perfect and in a rural area and cul-de-sac. Three bedrooms, fireplace, hardwood floors, privacy fence, garage, huge kitchen, and a big backyard. Big beautiful houses framed the cul-de-sac once I drove past the sign welcoming residence upon entering this well-manicured community. The schools the kids would attend were within walking distance, near to each other and immaculate. It was a breath of fresh air.

We got there by the afternoon. I Map Quested the address to what was going to be our new home and met the man who owned it. I got the keys and the kids immediately ran to pick their rooms. Right then, I was okay. A beginning to our beginning. I prayed, "Lord, I know you got me. I'm going to stick as close to You as I can. It's just me and You now as the two providers in this thing." Then, we began to live.

The Lord heard my prayer, which was sincere as I spoke it. The kids met awesome friends, they were free to go in and out of the house in the cul-de-sac to play with their newfound friends, walked to and from school freely, and were happy. This made me happy. Stepping into the unknown was one of the biggest leaps of faith. I learned that faith is sometimes something you have, even when you don't define it as such. When you aren't attached to Christ and take the chance at going into an unfamiliar situation, you are hoping and praying unconsciously over the outcome.

The difference was phenomenal. It gets better. It was just a realm of peace to not have to look around the corner for the next piece of pain that you hope isn't waiting to arrive. I was elated to move forward. The whole new life was a breath of fresh air. I was free to find a way for the three of us. I was ready to own walking into the unknown so that I could show our children that change doesn't always mean something terrible or forgetting where you came from or what you came out of. It means adopting a new focus and challenging yourself to see it through to the end so that the results are different and are a positive addition to your life.

I felt brave. Brave for disconnecting from toxicity or destructive infrastructures that caused a decline mentally, emotionally, physically, and spiritually. I'd taken the steps toward living and making things work. I loved where we were at that moment and my children were happy and that's what mattered.

I'd met people that were a great help for my children and myself with resources and an outpouring amount of support with small things needed. I nestled into our comfort zone and we made it fit what we wanted to happen along with being blessed to had found an area that was safe and immaculate schooling to boot.

I started feeling more independent on the inside. Reclaiming stability took me a little time, but my days were beautiful. I was bouncing back toward smiling, and watching my children laughing and enjoying themselves with their newfound friends was all I needed for strength. Learning myself all over again was a feeling of waywardness. Like even where to start in knowing what "I" liked to do outside of the children. I had to figure out what I wanted to do when they were visiting family or at school and it was just me alone. I had to reinvent myself. I had to find hobbies, try new things, think new ways, and meet people. I needed to get from under my safety net of only being a mother that kept me warm at night and proficient during the day. I didn't even realize that this was my hiding place for so many years until it was time to come out of hiding and the game Hide and Seek became real life for me.

I'd met people on the job I got at this medical facility only a few miles up the road from our home. Proximity played a great role in case something was to happen at my children's school or if I wanted to run home for lunch, I could. It was working out perfectly. After working there for a while, I'd gotten acquainted with the patient that was a regular. We became close friends as well as one of my co-workers. We all still talk to each other.

We grew a bond, and it felt as though I had been there all along. Going shopping at the Fresh Markets and watching my new friend cook because she was a chef. The dishes she'd make were unbelievable. Shopping and hanging out with our children were just what the doctor ordered. Things were great. My kids and I were planting our feet. It was the first time I'd been really on my own outside of my marriage.

I'd decorated our home very well and transformed our garage into the kids' play room with a huge black futon, game boards, an air hockey game, ping pong tables, a nice area rug in the middle, and put stuff up on the walls. Their friends would all come to play on the weekends or on some school afternoons. My daughter had gotten close with her classmates so much so that she'd be invited to slumber parties and, to my apprehension, I'd give in a couple of times.

We found a church home that was down the street from my job that was as big as what seemed to be three football fields. A well-known pastor I used to watch on television all the time was now where I was, physically standing in the sanctuary and joining his church. My kids became involved in different church plays and events and it was a true experience, to say the least.

I'd gotten close with the neighbors to where we'd sit on each other's porches to drink coolers and just shoot the breeze. It was nice. Getting to know others will show you that no matter what city, state or place you go to, we have all experienced life. My one neighbor who had lived in this cul-de-sac for years at first with her spouse had gone through a very messy divorce and she got the house with her children. The things she'd gone through were heartbreaking because of physical abuse being a huge part of things. She survived, she walked away, and she now had peace in her life. All the women I'd met had a story, and some were not so bad and others were worse than what I'd gone through. I found myself thinking, *Wow, I didn't have to go through all of that*, or *Even though I hadn't dealt with that, I dealt with what was outside of all I wanted to deal with*. There are so many stories and levels to a person's life, good, bad, or indifferent. Just listening to her talk about the nights of fear she endured, not knowing if that would be the day her life would end because the abuse was hurtful. In the end, we smiled over the memory because she'd survived and could live free of being afraid of anything. She was free to think, make moves and plan for her everyday steps without interruption or complications.

I would have never seen myself living that type of life in a million years. You know, living and breathing in peace. It was simply sweet and my sleep became easier and the thoughts and flashbacks were becoming more distant.

Me and the kids traveled to other parts of the state we lived in to visit family and spend the night. We toured the areas and enjoyed our new life. Enjoying all the festivities and main attractions was a big to do. As time went on after two years, the medical facility where I worked was closing and being bought out by someone else.

Looking for other work took a while and during this time, although the support given took care of the shelter, all other expenses to take care of all other necessities were out of pocket. It took a while for me to decide what to do because I really loved where I'd landed. We all know that whether or not work is at bay, bills will continue to flow. So, even though I loved the setup we got comfortable in, I'd decided to move closer to home as where we were was over nineteen hours away. We were okay where we were outside of my no longer working. As I was still trying to find my footing and felt I'd found it, I needed to change it. So, I'd made the moves to make it happen.

I would be closer to my mother but not right under her nose and I was doing great, but still vulnerable to finding that thing for us. I wasn't sure what that was going to end up being, but I was searching for it nonetheless. My intentions were not to drag my kids across the world and I knew that stability was what they were used to and what I was used to providing for them. I was still searching for solidity, so to move again wasn't easy, but necessary.

CHAPTER SIX

Life After Life Began

We moved to another location where there would be a shorter driving distance from my hometown. I had become more independent and still trying to find an anchor for the three of us. We settled in the state of Tennessee. Leaving our first stop was hard, but I took that leap and I'm glad I did.

So, our new place was where the kids would call their home. They'd become of age where friends were important, memories with friends meant a lot, school functions, etc., needing to be planted, stability in our situation was important and it was time to set roots for our new life. I confess I was still finding my way through mentally, but I was doing okay for myself.

Up to this point, we heard nothing from all I'd walked away from for two years. That hurt, but I dealt with it. From time to time, I felt sad because it wasn't fair that I wasn't able to live scot-free but had to scrape and struggle to make things work out. The one who ends things but continues with parental duties gets looked down on and the one who is free can script why freedom is at hand to anyone who will listen and buy the lies while the truth is making adult moves into living. Yes, I didn't have time to script anything because I was living my story step by step. I really was fine with this, though, because we were doing okay. Just needed to find that stomping ground that would be the thing we would remember out of everything and we'd found it.

Our children were diagnosed with asthma and one with asthma and eczema. I stayed up many nights from birth to school-age years, nurturing and nursing them back to being well. Sitting up while nebulizers ran, administering steroids to help keep lungs clear, Ibuprofen, Tylenol, and whatever else that was needed was what I did to handle all sicknesses that came about. Emergency room visits, school meetings, involvement in PTA and other things, clothing them from some name brand things to secondhand things and people giving me clothes, feeding them, and going without eating to make sure they ate. Like all mothers, I used child support given for the years I received it for exactly what it was to be used for and yes, it benefitted me as well, being that I needed to be under the roof, too, to raise my kids. It covered the shelter over their heads always and the rest came out of my pockets, such as utilities, toiletries, and all else needed to live. I got on any assistance there was with no hesitation or pride. As soon as it was permitted, my military identification card was deactivated, so I couldn't take the kids on base for continued medical care through the military. However, I found civilian doctors to take care of their health.

It stung; how unbothered the actions took to make this happen and how, for two years, it seemed as though the existence of ever having a whole family was ever known or shown.

I picked those pieces up and allowed the situation to resonate within me and placed it where it needed to be to move on. The kids and I talked a lot about what was going on later down the line. I was blessed that they were young enough to still be influential and having molding ability in truths, love, and old enough to understand that people are people and no one is perfect. I taught them that no matter what happens, it is always an individual's choice to make decisions in life and never to take the blame for other individual's choices, but to be true to whatever part they play in things. To be confident in themselves and to think through the choices they want to make before they make them.

We got situated in the house, which was a smaller home than the last home, but I still made it home for us. We always had our own rooms. The living room was small, the kitchen was a nice size, one bathroom, and I always had to have a backyard for them to play in. The kids got into school; I got a job and scheduled it around their schedules. Deep down, I knew God made things possible because everything fell right into place. He allows us to make decisions based on our plans but will make room for favor within the lesson we have to learn from our decision-making. It's inevitable because we will make moves He may not approve of but it is how we learn the difference between a hard and soft landing. When things just run smoothly, and no matter what the enemy does to throw a wrench in your footsteps, there is an invisible shield blocking any bad things from reaching you when you are connected to God. I know it was Jesus communing with the Father on my behalf. I received favor from people and situations that I couldn't have made possible myself.

He walked with me through it all and unbeknownst to me, already had my decisions made during this new life to meet His divine purpose for what I was getting ready to experience on this journey. It was going to be such a journey that would shape me and mold me into becoming who He needed me to become. Yes, I still slipped from time to time. I will never say that I'd arrived, and that I didn't make mistakes. On the contrary.

The house had a lot of issues with it, but I stayed for the length of the lease and then found another home that was more suitable for us. It was a lot bigger and had plenty of room for them to grow. It had extra rooms so I could space out things. It had a sunroom and a humongous backyard, too big to cut with a regular lawnmower. This was where we'd be throughout our being here together. Everything was so convenient to where my son would be going to elementary school and the bus picked him up and dropped him off right in front of our door. When it was time for him to go to middle school, it was right off to the left of our home, two houses down. My daughter's high school was right across the street. The area was beautiful, and I had good neighbors and we'd all looked out for one another. It was perfect.

My kids were happy with the new move and happy that they were making permanent friendships and had permanency and stability. This made my heart glad.

I no longer needed convincing that all would be all right. I believed it. I'd gotten a restaurant position and became the definition of humility for me. Our town was a suburban area that was a small, quiet, and quaint place that I labeled my own personal Mayberry from *The Andy Griffith Show*. Everyone spoke when they saw you and were friendly. It had a very low crime rate and was just a nice environment.

My job…well, I'd felt that I was too good to do this type of work with the skills I had. I'd always done office work of some sort or other type of work, so I broke down to tears when the lady said I'd gotten the position because it came too easy with no competition or challenges. This was a small town, with few offices, so anyone who held an office position wasn't leaving soon. Most of the jobs were in the bigger cities around this area and I needed to be where my kids were and didn't want to travel too far from them. This place was new to us and I needed to be close. All the while, God knew the plan He had and kept His hand in my life. Thank you, Lord.

This restaurant job fed us many times when I was low on food stamps or funds. For a couple of years, I'd ended up working this job and liking it because of the customers and employees. I was within walking distance when our van broke down and needed repairs or when it was fine and I just wanted to walk. My finances were sufficient to cover the necessities and I stayed thankful that we didn't face the lights going out or no water, etc. It wasn't easy, but for Him it was a piece of cake.

One day when I was at work and talking to a couple while cleaning off tables, there was a lady who was sitting at another table and listening to our conversation.

She called me over to her and said, "Hi, I just wanted to tell you that you have excellent customer service

"Thank you so much."

She then asked me had I heard of the company she worked for and I stated, "Yeah, I get a bill from them."

We both laughed.

"I think you would be a great asset to the company if you can do exactly what I tell you to do to become a part of the team."

I was thinking, if it's going to be a financial benefit, I was all in.

I'd done verbatim all she told me to do and within a couple of weeks, I was giving my two weeks' notice and starting a new job. Although it started off through the temporary agency that she'd called and set everything up for me, I was told that it would go permanent and I'd just need to be patient, but the payoff was going to be worth the wait.

The children and I celebrated, and I assured them that things were looking up. You would have thought it was Christmas, and we'd gotten each item on our list of wishes. We'd struggled. I'd have to say no to things they wanted to do regarding school, extracurricular activities as a family, etc., because it wasn't affordable. So, we were happy for a change of venue and even though we weren't getting ready to move on up like *The Jeffersons*, stability still looked better. Opportunities looked better and seeing the fight in them wanting to see things differently outside of what they were used to when they had both parents did a lot to my heart. Turns out, He gave me access to a better way of providing because of my humility.

We became more hopeful, saw promising progress, and remained humble. It was a helping tool to continue teaching them to always be thankful, respectful no matter what, and humble in everything. Later, I'd learn that although all I'd taught them were great lessons, it also was a crippling lesson. I guess I needed them to feel safe and stable minded in what we were going through somehow, but later down the line I needed them to not be passive aggressive but overtly aggressive with due respect regarding their feelings. There were constant lessons to learn when I think back on those days now.

So, here we were, a come up from where we had been and it was getting better for us. We began to see a glimpse of the light at the end of the tunnel. He was working while I was living this life by my thought process and learning how to lean on Him at the same time.

During this time of figuring things out in my singleness and single motherhood, I had been talking with an old friend from back home who I used to see back then and he now lived in the same area. As time grew, we started to see each other again. I needed that companionship to take different pressures off my mind. I needed to feel wanted. Besides, it was like my visiting a familiar place. My vulnerability level was through the roof and it was comforting to have had history already. I was enjoying the adult interaction with conversing and mingling. I was now working in a stable position that I confidently took on as mine and my house was in order with my children, so I saw the room to give myself a try at something personal for myself.

It was cool to catch up, laugh, and see where each other's lives had gone over the years. As we'd done this over the phone for quite a while before my getting to see him and visit with him after so many years had gone by. We'd talked about our lives and our children. Both having been married and now single and I was enjoying it because I felt normal again. I didn't have to focus only on my tasks at hand, so to speak. It became a plug that filled a space that had been void and lonely for a long time. Even though I was broken and hadn't totally healed, it was like placing those feelings on the back burner and living. An able body seemed better than nobody for me and I felt that this was even better because this somebody was that body that I'd already encountered. So, I thought "this" would be harmless. It was for me because outside of mothering, I had something just for me. Does that make sense?

Our conversations, in catching up, were awesome as we talked about back in the day and things we did while seeing each other back then—high school functions, dances, people we'd not heard from or seen in a long time, etc. It was great to laugh again and converse with the opposite sex.

We spent quite a bit of time together. He got to know my children and their interaction with each other was good. I'd never allowed anyone to get close to my children, ever. To even be in the vicinity of them, especially in the comfort of their home, was certainly a privilege. No one got to do this. We'd all travel back and forth to home for visits. I'd gotten to know his children. I was moving forward with my "new life."

I was defining a need and thought that it was a beautiful fit into all that was good without disturbing the characteristics of what was there already. I'd thought of the times when people added to their intimate circle (children and home) with someone other than the father, it could be risky. Most mothers are nurtures and protectors by nature and feel we can execute our needs and motherhood at the same time, thinking that the broken parts will somehow mend themselves during this process of self-satisfaction. The attempt for me was not to add to my situation or adding onto my damaged history, but just wanted a piece of special happiness. My kids loved having him around when he'd visit. Our families got together when we'd go home to visit and I enjoyed that.

Overtime, which turned into years, our relationship became not so fun and no longer full of laughter. I realized that I'd constructed a relationship built on my brokenness, which latched onto another's brokenness. We had learned of each other's history, and where we were, and who we were, and it just didn't fit together so much. When physical contact became a part of things, so did my soul tie to him, which became hard for me to let go of. I became dependent on filling my void. I allowed hurtful statements, spewed them back, dealt in dysfunctional events, chiseled away at my self-esteem through commanding love that I didn't have permission to possess or the broken promise from him telling me he would show me that all men weren't like what I'd left. The promise, in turn, was a fact that all men weren't like what I'd left but could be worse. It broke me even more. More so, I broke myself.

Broken wasn't defined as such at the time, even though it was present, but laid dormant. Time went on with the journey of having a great job, raising my children and thinking that I was functioning with added dysfunction by my own hands just fine.

My confidence in making it all work together somehow seemed justifiably plausible. However, the more I gave in at an intimate state, the addiction to it caused my walls to crash down. This was what physical contact did as I was wide open and shredded all the former hurt on to his doorstep, piling on top of what was already laying there. Even though I knew that during our living we had lives before encountering each other, because of the vulnerability and neediness state that I was in, I wanted the commitment. I wasn't about being the fly-by-night thing. So, learning about his life before me that was still active was hard and unacceptable but acceptable because I continued to deal with it.

I introduced the new me but he never saw the old me until it showed up and the broken wing I had bandaged was just starting to heal. After a long while of entangling with one another, I allowed the other wing to become broken as well. All the while becoming self-sabotaging in what I was now clinging to because it was supposed to be personally just for me and my personal space. Not noticing this, but God continued to work in my life. It was like He sat back and said, *I know she's fumbling, but she'll walk straight soon. I just have to get her there.*

CHAPTER SEVEN

❧

New Life. New Job. New Lessons

Windows were opening and blessings poured out of them, with doors of opportunities propping themselves up for me to walk through and take a hold of. The job I had was a predominantly Black company, that had great wages and health benefits when permanency was in place and I was happy to be there. I was willing and ready to work and show my capabilities, as well as learn new things on another level. I'd met some phenomenal people who were in upper management and gained a great professional rapport with them. My work reputation has always been what my mother taught me to have on any job. She taught me to be half an hour early because that was being on time, consistent, professional, ask questions, and not assume. As a child, I watched her execute these things by going to college when we were little and getting her bachelors and masters at Malcolm X College in Chicago, she became a part of the Board of Human Rights Commission, as well as several other boards, giving to those who needed help or just gave for no reason at all, along with being on other committees and saw how it worked in everyone's favor. Still, today she holds the same values as do I.

While working a great job now, I felt more secure. I felt more independent in taking care of things I couldn't before concerning

74

the kids and myself. My feet felt more planted. Although I was still a temporary employee, I got well acquainted with the area and on the job tasks. Outside of my personal life, it was smooth sailing toward the happily ever after I needed to be whole.

The dust behind my traveling from one of the hardest decisions I'd had to make when I left my marriage to this new place caught up with me. As I maintained a happy space for my children, worked and dealt with my own space of things with my friend. I didn't walk around looking like what I've been through. I'd smiled my way through old and new pain to remain stable in my blessing given. Each day I continued to smile through leaving one dysfunction while realizing I just picked up another one by choice. I simply handled myself accordingly, like a woman, and stayed on my grind at work. Working, mothering, and denying my part in adding to what was supposed to be in its healing stage. However, I had to place my hands in it to help God out because I thought I was entitled to a little something for myself while trying to heal.

I'd make it throughout the day in front of coworkers until I made it to the restroom and inside a stall where I could break down over dealing with the new hurt I inflicted on myself but was addicted and wouldn't let go of, for my fifteen-minute breaks, wipe my face with tissue, flush the stool which most times was a front, wash my hands, fix myself up in the mirror and would walk out of the bathroom door with the same smile I walked in with. I held this smile until I made it to my car and it was just me and Jesus.

Starting this job, I was who I was by a professional default. I always put my best foot forward to prove my professionalism, show consistency and make sure that being an asset remained the focal point and show God that He made no mistake trusting in promoting me to the next level. I was proud of myself. But how many of you know that with all the good accolades that happen, the enemy gets joy in stirring things up? It's as if you're too happy and that will never work. How dare you try to conquer what was supposed to be a loss? So, since you've added to what you thought you were finally getting free from, I'll add to it too and let's see you make it out of the storm. This is what the devil said about my steps because I opened the door too soon and didn't see that the adventures of me being happy, my household had needed a little more time before pushing the button to any additions.

I often asked God why things had to happen, especially when my initial reasoning and plans were on point without ill intentions and what I thought was right or okay to do.

The whirlwinds and hurricanes I was about to face no one could have ever proved a reality to me. New and old storms brewed while I tried to hold on to the calm before those storms, but the winds were brutal and aggressive at times with my maintaining the professionalism I was trained to have. Trained to become more than one person in my marriage became an attribute that spilled over into my single life and professional life. I had new upgraded masks of every facial expression that could fool nations. It was exhausting, but I somehow made it work.

During my journey on the job, raising my children, in and out of the relationship that I thought I was in and functioning on fumes of God and a whole tank of myself, holidays and different events came and went. On one Christmas holiday, the kids and I went home to visit and while there, we found out that their dad was at his parents. It had been a couple of years since they'd seen him or heard from him and they were excited and wanted to see him, so I dropped them off so that they could visit. I didn't get out of the car, but was happy for them to be able to spend time with the other side of their family. Over time, the part of me caring about what was going on with that end had gone and it wasn't about me more so than it being about them needing this.

This visit ended up with them calling me at my mother's and begging to stay the night over their grandparents and while I was a little hesitant, this was the inevitable. It was also nice to have a small break to myself and to regroup a little and spend time with my family and catch up on things. So, they stayed.

Things went immediately left once I called to see when to pick them up. They were taken out of town without my being consulted and I was told that I would not see them again. I had to call the police, file a report, showed them the initial court order of my having custody and they attempted calls numerous times with no answer. I panicked and was pissed at the same time. Other family stood there at the police station as well and as usual made excuses without seeing truths for what it was. Blaming and lying on me made it make more sense for them. However, I no longer cared what anyone thought of me. I wanted my children back, and this was all I was concerned about.

The last call the detective made was to make it known that if the appearance of our children weren't immediately displayed, there would be kidnapping charges, and they would be making a call to the military Command to report such heinous behavior. Over an hour later, my children appeared. I never saw this coming.

Upon them returning not even understanding the whole backdrop of being dropped off at the police station, it seemed as though they'd genuinely enjoyed their visit with the other side, and I was simply happy to see them. It wasn't important enough to me to put them through the bad parts of explaining what had happened and disregard their time spent.

Once we got back on the road to return home, when I asked how they enjoyed their visit, I was told of a woman who was there and that they remembered her from a long time ago. Our son seemed okay with it, however, our daughter wasn't so thrilled. She said that each time she wanted to get close to her father, the lady would take her space and made it hard for her to spend the time she wanted. Honestly, it crushed my spirits seeing the look on her face. Whoever she was, you had a whole smooth two years obviously that you had opportunities and free time so where was the respected boundaries with our children and the reunion?

I told her it was going to be okay and that no one person could ever take her place in her father's heart and made up an excuse for the situation. In my heart, I didn't even believe what I'd just said. They both also stated that he asked them if I was seeing anyone.

This was where my turn of events, storms, hurricanes, tornadoes, volcanoes, whirlwinds, and destruction began. I didn't see the tsunamis coming nor did I expect the ruins the answer to that one question would cause on so many levels that the phrase, *There's a level to this*, wouldn't even scratch the surface of the wrath that awaited.

My children answered the question and then said what no separated or divorced parent wanted to hear from their children about the other parents' new friend. They said that they loved my friend and that he was nice. No matter who started it, who ended it or what was going on in between, these words leave a very bitter taste in the receiver's mouth. For a minute I tasted the same bitterness as they talked about the lady being there during the holiday only because I was immediately curious as to which woman it could have been. Not because I was jealous. There were plenty of women to choose from, so of course, as we do, we try to visualize the person. I wanted to ask what they looked like or in my case I thought, could it have been one of the women I'd spoken with over the phone before? Either way, the taste that lingered from the other side came with a venom I would be poisoned by for years to come. I guess it was okay to move forward, but I was supposed to stay bound, alone, and regretful.

Overall, the kids had a good time. However, I was thinking, *Okay, they finally got to see him which is good. Maybe now they'll get to communicate more.* They needed the balance, and we needed to co-parent, but the stunt pulled had me questioning mindsets and the children being questioned about my life had me uncomfortable.

We arrived home, school was back in session, I was back at work, my situation-ship picked up where it left off, exchanging masks remained and my maintaining amid juggling things continued.

About a month after being back home from the holidays, I received a court order in the mail. The date of the order was filed in my hometown and it was an attempt to take full custody of our children. As many dysfunctional situations I'd gone through with misplaced parenting and marital skills, suddenly the need was felt to just take over. After moving on, thinking it was supposed to be a wake-up call for me, but didn't work, the concerns for who was in my life should have been the last thing that mattered.

At first, I thought, *Has everyone gone crazy?* The time that was missed being spent or communication with the children for two years had gone by and after a visit, this is what's conjured up? I didn't leave out of boredom or because I found a new hobby or new person. What type of person is it that finds joy in attempting to cause someone else's life to crumble when they initiated each crumb? Another wife and her husband shelled out gas money for our kids to get to school and dug down deep into their deep freezer to pull out food for us as if it were our personal food pantry when our joint bank account was changed to an individual account and I was removed. I could go on and on, but it's unnecessary. Really? Custody? This is when flashbacks returned and my anger arose. Then I had to laugh which was the only thing I could do because of the huge disbelief and trying not to snap.

Here I was getting on my feet with my job, maintaining stability, dealing with my own life choices and now this?

I had to figure out this whole court issue and how I needed to explain to my employer that I had to take time off work to drive eight hours to get to this court session. Not to mention my van had seen its days but it was what I had. This meant that I also had to rent a vehicle to even make it to this session. It was added tasks to my list of already eventful things going on and there was no choice but to handle it.

The most viable thing to me was to separate my personal life from my professional one. It was easier said than done. No way was I wanting my work life to know the dark secrets of what was going on once I clocked out for the day. Whether it was innocent or incriminating, it was a part of my private life. My past was my past, and I had no reason to think it would come back into my present. I had to get my thoughts together to contemplate quickly how I was going to do this without telling my life story.

I didn't tell my life story, but it doesn't take a rocket scientist to figure out that showing a court order to your employer wasn't a doctor's appointment. It was embarrassing, demeaning, and insulting. I didn't see it at the time because of intimidation, but this was what the enemy wanted all along. I became so intimidated by it all and mentally sown up in insecurities that my middle name was weakness and strength was far off for a good fight. But God. While I was feeling defeated, He stood in the background and kept me. Literally kept me.

My situation had become public knowledge and I no longer had a secret that only I, my circle of friends or family, knew and dealt with. The words the devil brought to me earlier on about having the nerve to open the door to moving too soon irritated my thoughts, but I had to rebuke it and move past the thought.

Each time I turned around, there was another court order in the mail for me to appear to prove the same thing and I had to rent another vehicle to drive back to my hometown. I was replaceable and disposable at my job and was being attacked by paper coming in the mail. Why all the complications and interruptions now? I didn't need this and was certainly okay with living our own individual lives as we saw fit. Why couldn't co-parenting and happiness for whatever we were personally doing be key?

God orchestrated the minds of my superiors that could have told me that my attendance was important and could have given me warnings and write-ups just to start a paper trail. I was being covered and didn't have the space in my mind to even recognize it from being in the unexpected head space of events. They could have said that because I had a lot going on that it may take my focus away from my duties so they would no longer need my services. This was an employer that was hard to get into where it took applicants two years or more to wait to be even considered for a position. They could have let me go. They could have counted me out. They could have written in my employee files that I was unreliable and would never be reliable or up for hire. BUT God!

It was like a balancing act on a tight wire rope. Balancing a divorce, trying to find my ground, singlehood, motherhood, dating, added stress in where I was going to keep getting money from for representation, renting cars, and my job. Internal daily thoughts about my life and blessings spanned throughout my nights, where I had lost a lot of sleep. I saw the blessings along with the hinderances, but didn't quite acknowledge the royalty in the blessing. It was a complete mess and I kept as best I could to maintain balance for my children. It was very hard, but all they knew was that we were going home more often and that they were getting to see family on both ends. Trying to keep issues away from them was so difficult from my reactions to things and my tears that sometimes I couldn't hold back and hide.

Somehow my past still participated in my present with spilled over vinegar that flowed into my day-to-day attempt to grasp for my future oil. We all know that oil and vinegar don't mix well.

Thinking of my job opportunity, I understood that because my steps seemed to be ordered even in my chaos, I owed this company a role that I had a part in and of an infrastructure that depended on my doing my given job. My possible permanent income was based on my performance. So, I had to leave my personal life out and chained up like a bicycle to a park rail because it wasn't wise to bring it inside. I mean, you do well in the beginning, being the new kid on the block and infinitely you are the mystery person. All eyes are on you to see if your capabilities can hold up to the standards given to you or expected of you. There is a window of who you click with and work relationships form and in comes the questions.

We've all been there where maybe we've been burned at a previous job and we vow not to make the same mistake on the new job as we did on the old by getting too close to co-workers. Is it possible to maintain the boundaries between work and home? I felt it was mentally, and I considered myself to be seasoned in learning what boundaries needed to be firmly set within the workplace. However, some feel as though work is "home away from home" and work relationships just become like family. This was just all too crazy to have even had to go through. Unnecessary.

I said all the above to say that while working my great position, I started as the mystery girl to some and, of course, to others it made no difference. As is with most places, some people just need to know your life story and others could either care less or it's on a need-to-know basis. My intentions were never to become an open book on my job. Those I got close with and comfortable talking to with answering questions and even volunteering information became a trusting ground. I learned that if there are no boundaries some things are set in discernment, however, the ones you trust are the same ones that share information at your expense. It was a huge lesson learned, but I'd grown to know that no one can tell your story better than you can.

I didn't have to state the reason for the court order, but that I had one and had to show up. When things become repetitious, however, it's kind of hard to keep things at bay and it became harder not to disclose my issues to my superior. Humiliating, to say the least, and it became quickly exhausting.

I was a wreck. I couldn't cover up everything that was going on by the way I dressed or my smiles, but the truth has always been more powerful. The truth was like my name, where it stuck to me like glue and became a permanent fixture. I was so weak and vulnerable and accessible to the point that it didn't matter where I may have wanted to go hide. I'd be found and exposed because a court order was a court order. Something I couldn't get around. Just as the Bible says that what happens in the dark will surely come to the light, truth is something we can never bypass to fool anyone, especially ourselves.

With every court order received, my anxiety grew. It was a mixture of knocking the wind out of me and feeling warm from sweat all over and anger. No one really knew my life or my story outside of the windows I opened to them pouring out bits and pieces. It was my paranoia that caused me to feel like everything was exposed. I don't know. I do know that a lot of nights I pretended my pillow was the shoulder I needed to cry on because I didn't have anyone that I was close to or no family to physically lean on at this time. I had my friend, but with all that was happening between us, I kept this part separate as much as I could. I couldn't bulk them together. It would have been too much.

Even though I knew why it all was starting, I still couldn't fathom why now? If it was about my moving on still. Why? When I left and it was stated that the infidelity was about to stop, I even called the bluff once I arrived home because I knew it was lie and said, "Okay then we will come back." Immediately he said, "No, you took it upon yourself to leave, so stay." Bluff called. I had no intention of going back, but just to prove that this newfound world meant more and there were no plans to stop. At that point, my worth was a fight that I'd become committed to battling through. It no longer takes anyone more than once to let me know they aren't that into me. I didn't know how I was going to fight through it, but it was staring me right in the face. Thanks to God for now knowing my worth and forcing someone else to see it is too much work when I learned I could use that energy to level up to a better me.

Level up to build a stronger platform out of the one I'd sweated and teared over with every new brick laid. Level up not to prove something to anyone else but to prove what was placed inside of me all along. Strength.

CHAPTER EIGHT

Court Proceedings

Having to rent a car, get the kids ready for this inconvenient trip, switch up plans for work and get mentally aligned with going to court was more than disturbing. To say I was nervous about losing my job would be an understatement. The people didn't owe me any loyalty. I hadn't been here for years to prove to them that my position was something they needed and couldn't do without. It was a horrible feeling to choose over a situation I didn't start and a job that was only to set things with me and the children on a better journey. The only positive side of this was that I and the children would get to see family and that we would get a break to visit.

The first court hearing had set the pace for what I now call my aggressive weather forecasts that continued to be unpredictable. No matter what I went through, my mothering could have never been questioned. Under no circumstances was that ever doubted until this point of pulling at invisible straws. My heart sunk at the accusation of my being an unfit mother. What a jab to throw and for what purpose?

While in court, the judge was only interested in what was best for the children, as is with most cases involving minors.

85

The lawyer found from the other side had to be found from the website: lawyersofthesamepersonality.com. Attitudes reflected were pompous, aggressive, and bullying that came across as if to say whatever was stated had to be the truth and nothing but the truth and would automatically win with the judge. Looks with threatening expressions and demeanors were stiff and sneakily underhanded. Walks with confidence, as if it were known right off things said would make good on achieving the sole purpose of this session.

Being that was the first hearing and my opponent appeared over the phone because of the job and I appeared in person, it went rather quick. The initial reasoning from the other side was to deem me unfit and the reasons behind it. Because both parties weren't present, the judge simply used that time to get clarity on the purpose of the case and stated that we needed another court date. The lawyer that stood in place of the absentee stated the reasoning for his presence that day was to gain custody for his client because it was felt that I was unstable and moving around too much. My lawyer explained the reason for my move was based on my leaving the marriage and finding footage and stability, which had only been two places and now was permanently settled.

The judge felt that if custody was the sole purpose, then both appearances were warranted and if it meant that much to the one requesting such a thing, their presence should have been a priority. So, he scheduled another date so that both parties would be present for a serious accusation such as this one. My palms hung sweaty, my thoughts were all over the place, and thank God I had my mother's friend as my attorney who talked for me because literally, I had no words that would come out of my mouth. Even if someone hit me on the back for me to spit them out, nothing would have come forth. I was totally speechless and in awe of the mountain formed in front of me. Utterly speechless.

A part of me was relieved. I didn't have to face my adversary. I had no desire to. I mean, what was I going to say or feel? I felt rage, hurt, disappointment, and harassed. This was a wasted trip outside of getting to visit. It was money I was losing from my job that I had no vacation time or sick to use. It was lessons from school for the kids and time in school with friends missed. It was a waste, and it was time to pack up and head back for the long drive home to put things back into perspective. This became like another job without getting paid for it after a while with each court date, renting a car with the little money I'd save up for any other rainy day besides this. Inconveniencing the kids with school absentees and feeling as though I owed an explanation to their being pulled out of school would soon be my part-time job. I drilled the importance of school in them and perfect attendance was always a reward they'd receive at the end of each semester of school since the beginning of them becoming school-aged. Not so much anymore due to interruptions.

I began consistently living my life on pins and needles because again, at the kindness of the woman who bought me into the company I was working for here, I was trying to convince them I was reliable and wanted to become a permanent employee. Attendance was of the utmost importance. Thankfully, that angel God assigned to me worked on the minds of those who had this authority over my fate. At this thought, I had to open up to my supervisor what was going on against my will. I remember thinking as I was opening the book to my life, would this person honor my personal issues? Would this person hold true to confidentiality? I was full of heaviness that weighed on my heart over this. However, I felt obligated to extend my explanations why I had to keep taking days at a time to go out of town. It was only right no matter what the outcome would be, because I didn't even know how long this was going to go on. He was more than understanding and extended his empathy, along with being more than supportive. Praise God! I didn't take that lightly, nor did I take it for granted. The pins and needles remained because even I felt that excepting my attendance level was being overextended and excused far beyond what the norm was.

While awaiting the next road trip, I went with my day-to-day routine knowing that this too had become a part of my routine. I started to pre-pack and made sure that I not only gave an account to my job as to all that was going on, but I'd given this same account to my children's schools. It was only right so that they didn't feel that my parenting should be in question as well. So, when I received a court summons, I'd let the school offices know by making copies of said summons so that my kids wouldn't miss any upcoming assignments or homework that would be due. This became an uninvited part of my life that bogarted into my space and I had no control of how long it would stay.

Even though the first court appearance was somewhat of an exhale for me because I was wound up way too tight with unawareness, I wasn't aware of the court's demeanor, what to expect, facing judges up close, or how to behave myself. I mean, what did judges look for when they faced both parties? I was at a total loss, but the first appearance was brief and kind of let me off the hook to get my grounding.

Up came the next court date, and I was a little more ready to walk in with familiarity to the surroundings and vibe of what took over a huge part of my supposedly moving forward. Mostly, from what I'd learned in my many sessions with the law, judges analyze each party. They pay attention to demeanors, personalities, and expressions, along with the relationships between the client and its attorneys. I've learned that right off in the beginning, they can assess who is full of it and who is trying to make it through it with some sense of victorious dignity. Immediately, I sensed this judge saw that the communication between the two of us was severed with no hope of repair.

The judge heard both sides of why we were there and set up a plan for joint custody. The court will do all they can do before they simply hand over the children because of an accusation against a parent. They do all they can to keep the children happy and stable and with familiarity. In most cases, it's the mother who goes through this and it may be because of the nurturing that's needed while the children are young or because it is just the right thing to do but the key is to give children what is best for them for where they are at.

I wasn't sure, but from what I witnessed was the fact that an accusation is just that from one party. It doesn't mean that it is gold and words set in stone and accepted. I know sometimes it doesn't work like this because of extenuating circumstances that some mothers find themselves in and may need to really get on their feet, but this situation wasn't that. Even then, judges may order children to be with someone else until things are better, but still are hoping to reunite children with their mothers. It's just a sad thing all around to have to go through. It was for me, especially when I had done nothing to deserve to go through it.

The court set up visiting times for the kids to go stay with the other parent every other spring break and every other summer being that we both lived in different states. I was trying to end something that I guess I felt was just out of anger and tried to stop it in its tracks. I tried to reason with the whole situation due to it messing with my journey as to becoming permanent on my job and possibly causing me to backslide into struggling again as we had when I was at the restaurant. I guess I was just trying to find any kind of way to stop having to rent cars, stand before a judge, and receiving court summons in the mail. So, with this, I volunteered to give him every spring and every summer visit and it was so granted. I was trying to execute a speedy remedy for the false purposes of my adversary. I wanted to show that regardless of the reasoning, we could simply put an end to this right away and agree to work with each other and co-parent. I felt it was a win, win. The judge agreed to my proposition, was impressed at the attempt to be open and giving, and granted it.

He also set up driving parameters, making it a fair driving distance between the two of us to meet and we set a reasonable meeting spot to exchange our children. This was too easy and went too smoothly without fire flames being thrown like the other lawyer seemed to have wanted to happen so, to add fuel to the fire thought to have had a win but didn't, falsely it was stated that I wouldn't allow the children to talk to their father when he called. He forgot to mention, of which my attorney took the liberty to do so, that there actually had to be calls made to have rejected such communication. I noticed the frustration in this judge's demeanor upon clearly seeing what was going on at that moment. The judge stated he was to talk to them upon calling at reasonable times that were convenient when the kids were home from school. He also wanted to meet in court again after the first round of visitations for the first spring and summer breaks for an update on how it went between visits and parental communication.

My lawyer told me before entering the session to not give any eye contact and to walk in with my head held high. She said that there was no need to feel anything about this case because we all immediately knew the reason behind it. She also said that when you know you know what you know to be true, there is never a reason to be defensive or shameful. Just tell the truth. Just being in there was intimidating and overwhelming, but I held onto her words and followed suit.

What she'd told me gave me a tremendous round of faith because she was absolutely right. I had no reason to feel bad and even though I did over the fact that we had to hold up courtroom time for nonsense, I held my head high because I knew our story. I was the one who chose to leave. I had nothing to hide, nor was I trying to prove a point because I was happy that our kids were able to see their family again after so long and I was attempting to show good intention by volunteering each spring and summer break. I thought that I was doing an honorable thing and was attempting to find some clarity and consideration in what I wasn't aware was a bomb timing itself down to all zeros and blowing up.

The other lawyer also attempted to use the time that was missed with our children as a crutch and tried turning it into a sympathetic thing. He stated that because of the military, there had been no time spent with the children in a little over two years and wanted to add more time with them outside of the given time for spring break and summertime. So, while we were there the judge ordered that our children get to spend time during Easter break as it would soon be arriving.

I had a job, responsibilities on keeping this job, and income that was just starting to flourish and not to mention a vehicle that was no longer long-distance driving savvy. I told my lawyer about this and she stated it to the judge with him still ordering the visit but stated, however, if there were issues on producing the children during this time, I was to let it be known to the other part and we were to come to an agreement over it. I looked at this judge and watched him look back and forth between us and it was like he wanted to try forcing some type of amends to see if it would work. He attempted to see if somehow for our kid's sake that we could start communicating with each other and come to a resolution that would make it work through respect between us.

He wasn't aware of the fact that we couldn't agree on it being daylight when the sun was clearly shining and it was noon. I got the notion during court that the judge picked up on this and all the tension showed, so he tried seeing if we could be adults about things and kept his order in place. He'd stated that if it wasn't doable, we'd have to come to another type of agreement by communicating. It consistently went south for the winter immediately when the times came. It was made crystal clear that things were set out for blood, no matter what was ordered or put in place. Communication was the last thing set on the table for the duration.

Seeing the one I'd loved and having had to leave brought back a lot of pain. I thought I was okay because it was an out-of-sight, out-of-mind thing for me. I took the air to breathe and would not have to look around the corner anymore for phone calls, proving infidelities, etc. I had freed myself from things, at least being right up in my face where these things were concerned. Being face to face again brought it all back into my heart and soul, and I had no words. Just my own bitterness without understanding the whys. Even so, I didn't take my bitterness out on the time spent with our children or the resurfacing of existence. I was okay and happy because of it since time had elapsed.

I pushed co-parenting to the front of the line for them and was all for it, even though it was hard to separate what I was being taken through. I had to separate my feelings from what I knew was right. I didn't want whatever this was that was in attempts at breaking me to win. The smiles on my children's faces made me overlook my feelings. I just never saw what my adversary was planning against me because of whatever had been picked back up from the heart.

It didn't matter about another woman or anything else like it was portrayed and displayed to be, it was really the other way around. That was a void thing for me because there weren't only this one but many and I knew already that even though the thought was that they could do a better job than what was told I'd did it just wasn't important to me. It never ends the way the outside person feels it will. This person had smirks on her face, as though just being present was proving something. The truth was, is that it only proved insecurities and showed the type of person they were desperately trying to be. Not secure in what may happen if they weren't there. There was totally nothing to worry about as I had no interest in being there or backtracking.

I'd understood karma and that it was real and God saw all. When you don't believe in what's right, you go for what it looks like. I was angry at that time for having been taken down that road for nothing. I had no idea what the punch line was supposed to be. We had been living just fine and growing as our own unit and I was open to having what they'd always known back in the picture as long as there was adulterated maturity in place. This wasn't the case, so I had to deal with what continued to be handed to me and I did it with grace as much as I could. I was just thanking God for my mother and my lawyer along with the fact that I didn't have to go through this lie of a case and ludicrous antics alone.

The kids spent time warranted with family after court, and it was time to go back home. I felt all kinds of things driving home. Thinking of what this whole thing was starting to look like, what I was going to do about Easter knowing that I didn't have ample transportation for the meet to do the exchange back and forth and my job. Money wasn't just laying around waiting for me to grab it for a rental or being dispensable to grant every distasteful scheme.

Easter came and, of course, I couldn't afford to take off nor had I had reliable sources of transportation, so they didn't go. I attempted to do what the judge ordered, and I called to communicate and make it aware that I couldn't afford things. The whole thing was blown up saying that I was doing it on purpose and that the other lawyer would immediately file a motion to prove I was in contempt of court. It was forgotten about what the judge said in the end of the last session, obviously about trying to work it out if I couldn't make it. So, I was unbothered over the blow-up.

It was called and reported that I didn't present the children for the holiday and a summons was received in the mail from papers being drafted up for court, stating as such. It stated that I was going against the court order and that I was in contempt with big red stamped words all over the subpoena. All attempts to harass and bully the situation and to make it out to be anything other than what it really was. Nothing came of this as the judge continued in his attempt to see the two of us work our disagreements out. He didn't even call for a court session regarding this bogus summons and I was happy about it. Unfortunately, communications went unsuccessful. On top of the summons being ignored by the judge, there were still this motion filed with red stamped words all over it and that motion filed and mailed to me as if to show me the aggression that was going to take place no matter what and even though every attorney had the right to file it, it all was overturned and dismissed. This attorney was like a pit bull that was always hungry and was never getting enough to eat.

Spring break came soon after the Easter holiday and because I was aware of it and able to prepare for it, they were driven the halfway mark to the meeting place and the children were exchanged. The first time, it felt weird and felt like I wasn't living in reality, but living a movie that I've seen all other families go through but couldn't possibly be my life. Summer came, and I did the same thing. It felt the same as the first time and I soon saw how it seemed my life was going to be for a long while until our children grew older. What an interruption this was and for what?

I felt bad for our children because they didn't ask for this. I also, at one point, found myself wishing that the disappearing act would've remained a permanent thing and continued living this supposedly best life. Why did the past have to come and pour salt into wounds? Why did it feel as though what was good for it to move forward wasn't good for me, no matter what package it was in? I was supposed to rot and succumb to nothing? What were my children thinking about all of this? Why was the venom so poisonous toward me when all I did was leave?

During the time of their visits, I noticed our daughter was changing as far as her attitude each time she'd returned home. Our son seemed to be just fine. I learned from my son that the treatment between the two of them was being handled differently to where our daughter was being treated in a not-so-positive way and our son was being favored a lot. I wasn't sure what this was about and I could only wait until she came back home again to talk. She'd stated that the interference was from the one who entered uninvited a while ago but stuck around for their own personal agenda. All decisions were made through that person and it was simply agreed with as if it were a set rule to agree amongst each other, no matter what.

My daughter had written a letter which I still have about the treatment received, but she'd written that she still wanted to give it a chance. I know she wanted to gain back her own personal stance in this whole situation, so I understood. However, I made her promise me that when it gets too unbearable that she would say something and not keep it in. I'm not sure if it ever reached that point or she simply smiled to assure me she would, but kept it in anyway. I just prayed over her while she was away. I had to report it to my attorney so that she could bring it up in court.

We were given another court date to return after this trial run of events to see how things worked out with the order given. Praise God, my job continued to be understanding and allowed me to go with no issues.

It was like the more feathers that could be ruffled by sending all these letters notarized on every move I would make, even if it were small along with a copy sent to the courts and myself, the more chaotic things got. If the kids had events at their schools and phone calls weren't connected, I received a notarized letter, and copies went to the courts aggressively stating that I continued to be in contempt of court. It was awful. I realized that the goal was to have me thrown in jail as it was finally stated at one of the hearings that I continued to be in contempt when the truth was, my opponent took on this role but hid behind statuses. It was tried as hard as possible but was never successful. But God!

The lengths in trying to come up against me were endless and some of it would be beyond anyone's belief. It was something that I would never wish on anyone. Not even my worst enemy.

Unsuccessful in the contempt orders being served caused other drama under the radar. With our exchanging etc. there was a lot of drama involved upon meeting. At times, my friend would go with me and during these exchanges, nothing was said to me and we were simply able to do the switches and move on. During the times that I went alone, there was always a reason to approach my car and attempt to say something to me, but I wouldn't allow it.

On one occasion, the kids were already in the car after the exchange for their visit as I'd gone alone. I was approached again, and I immediately rolled up the window. My reasoning for not ever wanting to converse was because the looks I received were always rage and I never felt safe or comfortable.

I kept my window rolled up at this time and there was aggression in trying to say something and I had to shout out to move from my vehicle, but my requests continued to be ignored. I warned again to move back so that I could go and still no retreat. So, I drove off thinking that there was enough space to do so, but when I looked back all I saw was a lot of hopping up and down. I'd ran over a foot. With this and knowing the history of the relationship, I drove and searched for a police station because anything that could be used against me to have me incarcerated seemed to be at the forefront. Finding the police station, I reported what had happened and my situation, and unsurprisingly, they'd already received a call and reported it stating that charges were requested and had a video to prove the incident.

This whole thing was crazy. Here I am in a whole other state and away from home at this police station nervous because I know I didn't do this intentionally, but not knowing what part the video showed, I wasn't sure of my fate. Once the police saw the video that was set to be incriminating toward me turned out to be reversed and the truth was seen from beginning to end. After reviewing it I was told that I did nothing wrong. What was to be the sure thing that would have me arrested only backfired as it showed my car being approached with me requesting them to move away, so I was not deemed in the wrong for leaving and was seen as someone trying to avoid confrontation.

This, along with many other dramatic issues, was directed to the courts but with information left out as to the initiator and more received notarized letters in the mail came for me on being in contempt and court. Summons for new attempts to prove our children were better off without me would pile up and it became so much that yes, I broke down more than I want to remember. I was being bullied through the mail and at first; it was more than overwhelming and caused a lot of emotional distress, but after a while, I saw it for what it was. Unhappiness. Still, it had a huge effect on me and was causing things that I would or could not even explain to anyone.

All this time with going back to court for the updates was stressful. I wasn't sure what was going to happen. Hiding behind the military was used more than none each time using this as one reason for something or never abiding by the orders given behind filings that weren't submitted by me to begin with. The judge simply continued to work out this situation without tampering with the sole custody issue and wanted it to remain joint custody. He tried extremely hard to work things out between us. It was never reciprocated to find a common ground so the attacks continued through the mail with notarized papers. It got to the point where I dreaded going to my mailbox because I was so tired of seeing court orders and contempt letters.

In all these issues I remained KEPT and it wasn't easy for me to realize it and grasp onto the favor given. Sometimes my children witnessed me snapping over the phone and going off saying things that my limit that I was at called for. It was insanity and unfair. No matter what, I needed this to be my winning that was going to end up looking more like peace and not war. I was sick of this and wanted it to end.

CHAPTER NINE

One Session Down,
Unsure of How Many More to Go

When wanting sole custody didn't work and joint custody was ordered and set. This was done at the session with an update as to how the visits went and were there any change in adult communication. Of course, I'd had my attorney mention the difference in treatments between my children while visiting and the concern it raised. It was noted and we had to get on the stand to report to the courts our stances on things.

At this court hearing, I was accused of being on drugs and was seen coming out of a known drug house in the state I lived in. The judge asked if there was any proof like a video or something showing this hearsay as it couldn't have been a personal witnessing being that we were living in two entirely different states. The reply was that a friend who lived where I did just happen to see me coming out of the house that was well known for drug activity and the friend called to report this out of concern. This wasn't considered solid proof, but the judge was thinking about the best interest of the children so he wanted to do a home study to follow up.

I guess I was bothered by the fact that this was even entertained and a home study was needed. Suddenly, I was the worse mother in the world from having the nerve to have someone else in my life who continued to be a focal point throughout our court appearances, never having once met the man to being on drugs. Statements made from the stand at this session were that while the children were visiting, our daughter had issues with her personal hygiene and that it was said that I never taught her anything so she had to teach herself. How unstable I was mentally due to the miniature seizures I'd had back when our daughter was born and it affected my thinking abilities with making decisions. Oh, that was it for me. How hurtful it was to use something that almost took my life bringing life into the world and not to mention a baby that had both DNAs attached. Really?

At once upon this being spoken, my lawyer had to hold my forearm because I tensed up and was ready to call all the ball face liars out for what it was right there in court and add some choice words to boot. This session was a skit out of "Let's just make stuff up as we go" and an insult to the judge's intelligence as though he'd never seen this happen before. I watched this judges' facial expressions and body language as I'd learned to do during previous sessions, just as I knew that he analyzed all parties of the courtroom. He already knew that it all was bogus but he humored it sort of speak with ordering the home studies. What wasn't so humorous, however, was that he wasn't aware of the time that had already been extended to me to be off work to handle such a monstrosity of events. What was also not so humorous was the fact that people who never knew me were commenting on things as if they'd been there all along but were only going by what was told to them. They forced their spot in the limelight and weren't even relevant in my eyes.

I took the stand and was questioned about my life and our children's. I spoke of us attempting to move forward after leaving.

Questions were asked of the reasons I thought our presence was mandated in court at that time. My answer was that it was out of bitterness out of my leaving and because of a question asked during a Christmas holiday and I'd referenced the question and the answer from my children that was given. I'd stated my actions were legit and I never looked back but couldn't have ever imagined the outcome of it. I'd started to use such a situation as bringing life into the world and the repercussions of it was more than sad, it was ignorant and hateful. My attorney bought forth evidence of being harassed by mail while I was on the stand and produced the wedding invitation that was mailed to my home and the picture of a wedding ring sent to my phone. An invitation that my daughter opened happily thinking it was something else but it was a formal invitation and, on the inside, where both names were printed, one last name was scratched out and replaced with the name that would be given once it was over. Across the top, it read: **You are Cordially Uninvited to Our Wedding.** The place of the event was torn off at the bottom. The only issue I had with it was that my daughter read it and wanted to know why it arrived in that way. It left me to try to explain the best way I could to a child. Other than that, the contents of it made no difference to me. I'd already played that role and had I not walked away from it there would be no invitation to send.

When questioned about it, the other party lied and stated that it wasn't sent by them when the postmark clearly showed it coming from the same place of residence. After it was made clear that it was indeed from them the judge scolded the tasteless and tacky move. He stated that all parties involved should be ashamed of themselves. This all was just ridiculous and a waste of everyone's time.

So, the order was to go through Domestic Relations Bureau counseling screenings ordered by the judge in his attempt to continue seeking some type of remedy with our communication skills and common ground. Looking back on it all, this judge had to have a soft spot for family and peace between parents. He really tried all that he could to see if we could come to some sense of humanity and let the past things go and try to co-parent bless his heart. All while he attempted this, his entire demeanor continued to remain calm, soft-spoken with a low tone in his voice with each session. Even though his efforts never bought forth the outcome he was reaching for I really appreciated it. I'd had the same hopes so that my life could get back on the track it had been striding on and the room to mend within myself, all I'd had going on alone without this extra to deal with.

Upon returning home even though there was no proof to the allegations of my being on drugs I had to do an in-home screening with the Bureau of the state. Another day off work and with this type of appointment I had to take the children out of school so that the Home Visit Agent could talk to them too. We both were ordered to do the same in-home visit with the Domestic Relations Bureau in the respective states when the kids could be present so on their next break was when it would be done with the other party.

The Case manager came and sat with the children and me and was impressed with the décor of the house. After speaking with her she was at a loss as to why we were even in this situation and once she spoke with the kids as she took them away from me and into our backyard, to speak with them alone she was convinced. She stated that despite her personal assessment of things she had a job to do. She stated that while speaking with the kids she asked them how they felt about everything that was going on and she said that they both stated that they wanted to see their parents back together but knew that it wasn't going to happen. They wished the arguing would stop. She then said she asked them how they felt about living with me and they said that they were happy and loved their school and friends.

She needed to see the kid's grades which were always A's and maybe a couple B's and C's but nothing below this. We talked about the underlying reasons that I was going through this and she stated that even though there was nothing to really report negatively she still had to make sure things were done thoroughly. I understood this.

She asked about the relationship I had with the other parties involved and I'd stated to her that I didn't have a relationship with them nor was I in any type of ill way over it besides what's being done toward me through court. I'd stated to her that I've been trying to live my life without interruption and move on. I told her that suddenly I was receiving wedding invitations and pictures of wedding rings to my home that wasn't needed and showed it to her. I told her that after seeing the type of person this was, I had no desire to have a relationship. I told her all that I'd dealt with up to the point at hand and was simply exhausted. After the meeting was over, she said she had to make a report and turn it into the courts and we'd go from there.

The report from the other side was as animated as expected with exaggerated scenarios trying the hardest to prove my being unfit. I was able to read the report after it was all turned in and both attorneys were sent a copy of each one. The report stated that I really had a substance abuse problem because of the drastic change in my appearance. I thought, "Wait, what?" There were quotes from our children saying that they didn't want to be with me and felt safer on their visits and never wanted to leave once they came for their breaks. The report said that the year our daughter was born and that after her birth I'd suffered a stroke that caused brain damage and since then I'd become confrontational and irritable all the time and said that after the ship went out to sea that I couldn't take care of our daughter alone so I had to go live with parents that weren't mine because I didn't have any help from anyone else.

A lot of other things were stated like while supposedly living with in-laws that I had to go through Rehabilitation while in their care. Reports that at times I was hard to locate because I moved around too much and no one could ever find me. I had to laugh at the reading of this because maybe the thought was that I was never going to see it or hear about it. There was so much lying going on that the truth about the birthplace of our son was given wrong and that at this time we were on sea duty when in fact we were on shore duty the whole time until we left to go to another duty station. The date of our son's birthdate was even given wrong. Desperation will often cause forgetfulness and confusion. I still have this report to this day as well. I know it's time to trash it all and maybe I will one day. I guess having it shows the endurance I was given and got through and the strength to empower others with my story. It reminds me that no matter what comes down on you, you can still forgive and move on.

Lies went on endlessly in this report. At that time, I was livid, humored, insulted, hurt, sad that there was so much hatred toward me in it, and plain exhausted over the whole thing. Each time I'd go to my mailbox a lump would form in my throat from anxiety upon possibly receiving another court summons of some sort. Knowing that I still had to go back to court, I always had to figure out how I was going to keep taking off work and not lose my job. Constantly taking the kids out of school was more pressure than none. No matter what, it had to happen. The next court appearance was to be an important one based on the answers of the reports turned in, so everyone had to appear rather they had work or anything else. Mind you, during all this time I am still but a temporary employee at this company.

Once this report was turned into the courts and I awaited the decision of the judge over my being deemed unfit to continue caring for our children, I prayed. I prayed that God would touch the hearts of those who tried so hard to come up against me. I prayed that this all would disappear and we could all just go back to living our lives. I prayed that He would keep me sane and hold me up while dealing with this fiasco.

Nothing came of it so again the attempts went unsuccessful. Even so, it seemed as though losing became fuel and every time I sneezed, I was receiving another court summons in the mail stating that I was in contempt of this or that when a phone call was missed due to them having extracurricular activities after school or if we had family plans to go out. The calls that were made weren't nearly close to the ordered times that the courts offered and because we didn't sit by the phone waiting for it to ring caused there to be reason to file contempt charges against me. If I were a minute or two late pass the time at our meetup place after a week would go by there was another contempt order mailed.

During these contempt orders and due to the cost of traveling, my attorney stood in and showed up for those court appearances on my behalf to dispute those orders. One contempt was filed stating that when the children were able to talk on the phone, I was always in the room while conversations were being had with the children and it was deemed as a distraction and interruption. My attorney contacted me and conveyed to me that the judge ordered me to leave the room when they had their phone time. Me, leave the rooms that I furnished and dwelled in just to save face. Yeah, okay.

I'd received a summons on amending child support or custody modifications, staged voice mails between the two of us were played in court by which was mysteriously sabotaged somehow by only playing the angered remarks I'd made and responding remarks went missing from the recording. My Facebook page was presented in court at one hearing. Screenshots were taken on things that felt would help regarding posts I'd made venting about hate. If I went on a vacation to clear my head and shared pictures on Facebook, this was used saying that it was where the child support was going toward instead of taking care of our children. This type of behavior continued no matter how much I tried to co-parent and prove that these summonses were bogus and bullying. Still, I had to constantly rent cars, take the kids out of school, take time off work, and travel out of town for these same bogus summonses when ordered to.

CHAPTER TEN

Mental Rollercoaster

Things started to affect me mentally when shenanigans and attempts to harass me continued to happen off the grid and outside the courtroom. I thought, *My leaving was supposed to be the start of my life and the end of what I no longer wanted to keep in my life*. It turned out to be worse after leaving than when I'd stayed longer than I desired. I felt trapped and in something I couldn't get out of and was uncertain how long I would be detained in this trap.

During proceedings between court appearances, I received unwanted home visits unannounced with demands to see the children. I'd requested this presence to leave as we made no plans, nor was this wise being that we were going through the courts. I threatened to call the police and once I had my phone to my ear, I got the middle finger and a tongue licked out at me followed by skid marks after driving off. I still made the call to report it and described the vehicle. Because there was no physical altercation, I couldn't do a written report, but verbal was good enough for me. At least I'd reported it.

After this, calls were made to my local police precinct, making false reports, stating that due to being in the military he felt our children were in danger and asked if someone could check on them since he couldn't personally do it. He gave my address and they'd come to investigate, finding nothing out of place or in harm's way. This was done numerous times until it grew tiresome on their parts. So, the police officer came once again, but this time it wasn't to investigate. He stated they had reason to believe (this after the first time when I explained motives and the pattern was proven) that false reports were indeed being made and the captain of the precinct warned that if the calls kept coming, they would contact the Commanding Office of the military about this behavior. The calls stopped.

Calls were made to my girlfriend to talk to her about me and the person I was seeing, saying to her, "She must really like him a lot." Consistent calls to plead his case for some reason made it seem as though it would make a difference. I'm not sure what he thought would come of this. In the beginning, I was unhappy with it, but then I let it go because no one knew the truth besides three people. God was the third party. I knew only God had the power to make a difference in this situation. After a while, I had to get myself under control and all I wanted was to co-parent. It was tough to transition with all the antics and I couldn't get over one thing before another thing would start. But I did.

During one school season, the principal called me at work to report that they had a visitor come to the school and tried to check my son out. She stated that the appearance was in military uniform attire and felt this was going to make a difference. She'd stated that there was a repugnant demeanor, as if they were supposed to jump at a "ten hut" position upon appearance. I only had myself and a friend's name listed on the checkout list. For years, there weren't any interests regarding their schooling or inquiries about how they were doing, along with the fact that we didn't even live in the same states, nor were there any involvement in their schooling. I had given each of my children's schools a copy of my court papers stating that I had custody and under no circumstance was anyone to take them without my being notified. This was madness beyond madness to feel as though whatever was desired to do was at the feet of standing behind a uniform. No one jumped to this military status, and no one was checked out.

Since the local police department didn't execute the intentions that were in hopes of, and the school would oblige, calls were made to CPS (Child Protection Services) with the same accusations. Again, more proof that I had to show that there was no problem at my home or with the kids. With this being reported to CPS I had to take off work to go in person to have an interview with a caseworker and then an appointment for them to come to my home to do the same thing that the other agency before had to do. Meeting with my children meant more time out of school.

These things continued to be done under the radar of court. The ones who kept causing the summons to come were causing the most hell, harassment, and mental torment. Upon involving CPS, the first home visit comprised the caseworker walking through my home, looking in my refrigerator, my cupboards, closets, underneath beds, and had to take pictures of my children by having them lift their shirts to take pictures of their stomachs, arms, and legs. Feeling totally disgusted, I saw rage. I felt violated, disrespected, and living a bad dream that had no end. At times, I started to backtrack and question myself and my own motherhood. Trying to look at each step I'd made at the beginning of their births. I started doubting myself and questioning everything I would say to them or did even. This thing started placing fear in me at possibly losing them. It was pure chaos knowing that I'd done nothing but feel like I'd had.

The caseworker that came was an African American young woman who was medium height with beautiful blonde dreadlocks. Very well-groomed and very down to earth, which made the visit easier to get through. After she took the pictures, she stated that there were no noted issues she could see. She then needed to speak with the kids just as the lady from the Bureau had to do. After speaking with them she said, "I have been doing this for a very long time and can tell if the house has been cleaned just because of the appointments made by us. By the looks and upkeep of this house and after hearing even your children speak and being so well mannered, I can tell you that the person who made this case against you must be pretty angry with you." Of course, this bought on a debriefing of my background. She couldn't tell me who made the phone call, but I told her I already knew who it was and that she didn't need to tell me.

She said to my children, "You both have great grammar in speaking, there are no bruises on you and you live in a beautiful home with a huge backyard and you'll never know how blessed you are." She told them she wished she could take them to homes where true neglect and abuse was happening and how most of the kids don't have beds, a big backyard, a kitchen full of food and can even speak as well as they did. Then she told me that even if it is a false allegation, unfortunately, there was nothing I could do to stop the calls besides report it to the courts because upon each call, they must fully investigate no matter what. But God!

I'd have to leave work, take the kids out of school three more times after this for the same issue with Child Protection Services. The fourth time, the caseworker called me to say that they'd received another call but they have found that with all the findings of them coming to my home to find the same outcome ruled it as a person only trying to build a case against the accused.

She said, "We aren't going to ask you to meet with us anymore and you don't have to take time off work or take the kids out of school, but we have to drive to the address to say we investigated behind the call. I will just sit in front of your home and note that I came and then leave. You don't have anything to worry about." I praised God at that moment in tears because folks even though I knew that there was never anything they would or could find wrong, my mental state was going toward broken more than the shattered pieces it was already in, and crying just wasn't cutting it anymore. I'd cried enough from the unfairness. I'd cried enough from lies and intimidations. I'd cried enough. Still, I cried.

With all these things done, with the courts having no idea of the events happening until we returned to court, I still had to honor the court order and allow our children to visit for the summer that was approaching. We met at our meeting place and exchanged the children. I couldn't do anything but wait until my attorney could report these actions to the court when we reappeared.

The time was approaching for our next court proceedings from both Domestic Relations Bureau reports and now the added report from Child Protective Services were entered. This was the hearing that the judge called to go over everything that had been brought in front of him from the beginning. Not being aware of the activities that had taken place between court appearances, my attorney was more than ready to bring them into play.

I was just over it all already. It just seemed as though no reprimands were put in place and I'd gone through volcanic emotional combustions. During this session, all reports and behaviors were produced and the opposing attorney had no defense to what he was unaware of as well. He had no idea of the extracurricular activities his clients were doing. His facial expressions said it all. I think he was tired of fighting over what became very plain and obvious to him, too.

The judge read both reports over before court started. After hearing all that had transpired with paperwork for proof from my attorney while waiting for this day to arrive, he found that our case was very saddened in his opinion and that all he felt was compassion for our children. He also stated that he could find no just cause to deem me an unfit parent and would not find in favor of handing over sole custody from under me, but would continue the order for joint custody. Embarrassed at even being connected with such activity, I agreed with him.

Along with this, my attorney had advised me to get letters of recommendation from co-workers and this is what I'd done. I had the letters stating that my permanency was a sure thing, but that it was a process. My being temporary and blessed to continue working after all the absences for court was nothing short of the intervening of God. It was a good gesture, but all in all, to the judge, it was still just a letter with no solid results. It was a promise that had not yet been executed, so he still had a job to do in his concern regarding standing stability financially over my children.

Over the disappointment in the judge's ruling, the opposing attorney brought up the fact that I was only working a restaurant job and a temporary job and that it showed instability. He didn't even know the true facts about what I was doing.

However, with this, the judge asked to explain my situation. I corrected the partly false information and stated that I was given the opportunity at a great position and had been temporary for almost a year, but in a few months was assured permanency. I stated I worked extremely hard at taking care of our children in the absence of the other parent from the day they were born and that it hadn't changed now. I worked at a restaurant because I needed to do what I had to do and had no reason to be embarrassed about working temporarily toward putting things back together stability-wise for my family. Afterward, the judge appointed us to come to yet another appearance, and the last one four months from that time and at the time of the hearing, I would have to have gained permanent employment. He stated that if at that time there was no stable work on my behalf that unfortunately, he would have to rule over giving "temporary" sole custody until I could find permanent stability.

He made sure to let it be known that this decision was not a personal choice of his but by law temporary work was not considered stable work and even though it was full time, it would need to be permanent full time and I needed to do what I could before the next court hearing to obtain it. He also stated that he felt he would be doing a disservice if he didn't respond to the outlandish behavior displayed between court hearings. He said that being a representative of the United States should have more tact and that he was disappointed at the vigorous attempts to take away any peace in our children's lives by turning things upside down. He lastly stated that he was not pleased with the behavior by no means.

You would think that this would have given me some great, "Yeah, you tell them judge," moment, but it didn't. It hurt, and it was a sad case, as he'd stated. My heart dropped. I felt like a criminal who had broken thousands of laws by even being associated with it all. Like I did something indisputable and could never be forgiven. Even though I knew I'd done nothing wrong, I questioned the whys in the back of my mind. It was just all so unbelievable. It was more anticipated time, more unknown outcomes, and more exhausting days and nights. This was the tell-all, and I wasn't given the spirit of fear, but it crept up within.

No matter what, it was never about tearing one down because I wasn't coming up against anyone but trying to live. For me, it was about healing and speaking it out loud to move on and let go. This was the hand I was dealt and should feel proud to state it but even today the thought of having gone through it and even things that went on currently in my life through these same emotions of coming against me still leaves a sadness in my heart. I don't have to pay it attention now and there are no reactions needed toward the heart of man, but it's still sad.

CHAPTER ELEVEN

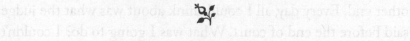

God is Good All the Time, and All the Time God is Good

During these events, I kept thinking, *Lord, I'm so tired. Fix this.* A part of me wished and hoped all sorts of things just to bring the quietest moments back with no drama. The children and I were just learning how to live life together and get through the change of things. Even with my adding to my personal life, this trumped anything I'd ever dealt with. I could walk away from my additions easily but didn't because of my insecurities and neediness for something I thought I needed. Life doesn't lead you; you lead it and whatever cards are on the table is the hand you play until you get better at the game and understand the rules. The lessons from those rules you gain are up to you to change the course or stay on it from being afraid to change. I was ready to change. I was ready to learn what it was I was to learn and move forward. Looking back on things I allowed and/or didn't ask for, I've learned and changed my course. This situation had taken a physical and mental toll on me to where only God could understand. How do you feel defeated by the truth?

Being back at work, trying to focus to be productive in my position, praying every day that they would decide to change my employment status, and some days wanting to just ask them to without exposing the reasons, my nerves were getting the best of me. It was like being a human hourglass being turned upside and down but trying to beat the odds before all the sand reaches the other end. Every day, all I could think about was what the judge said before the end of court. What was I going to do? I couldn't make my employer do what I needed them to do, even though my supervisor knew my entire story and what I was up against.

I was so weary of fighting. I was worn out, wondering about a fate that I hadn't even caused. I was exhausted at the fact that all I had done was be a mother to my children and a great one at that, but was being punished for it. On most days I felt numb and other days I felt nothing at all and just wanted things in this calamity to be over. My attorney assured me it was all going to be okay and all I could think was, *That's easy for you to say when you have nothing to lose.* It hurt the pit of my soul at the thought of me losing in a war where, through it all, I'd been the one who kept waving the white flag, trying to call a truce.

Four months went by as days and time were approaching for a return court appearance and I was not offered a permanent position. I was sick. Having to seem normal at work and be a functioning mother at home was tough, but I did it. I leaned so hard on God that I could have smelled his breath on my cheeks. I did because He was the one who kept me standing without breaking. Yes, I broke, but He wouldn't allow me to shatter. He even kept pointing out my decision to rush myself in, not wanting to be alone and dangling the current so-called relationship in my face. Even though I ignored it and kept moving forward He continued to tug at my heart with truths. To be in something that you know it's time to leave, you stay because the strength given naturally doesn't play a part nor does it win against flesh and selfishness. A part of me was selfish, even amid a lie staring me in the face that had no intentions of committing nor did it put salve on my wounds. It kept reopening them, but I kept putting a bandage on it to keep from seeing it.

Before this last court appearance, I couldn't sleep. It seemed I cried every minute I wasn't in front of the kids or at work because here we were, getting ready for this court date and I was still a temporary employee. I couldn't even confide in friends. My heart and mind were so full I had no words to converse with anyone. It felt like time was standing still and moving fast at the same time.

Each day, my heart stayed on my sleeve. It pumped fast and beat hard. I looked at the children daily, kissing their cheeks daily, and trying to love on them extra in those days because I wasn't sure about this ordeal. Talking to them and being honest with what was going on went easy because it was something that I couldn't avoid. I wanted them to know that no matter what happened, we would be together. On the inside, I prayed I was right.

Finally, the day to travel back home had arrived. I remember how sick I was and scared to even make this drive. After renting another car and getting my children ready for this trip home for court, I took the longest shower known to man that morning. While in there, I closed my eyes and pictured being away under a huge waterfall that sounded like how a massage would feel, with nothing but flowers and beautiful glistening rocks that towered around me. Calm streams, soft air, and silence from hearing anyone talking to me. As I was under the waterfall, I flashed back to when I first had my daughter and then the time my son was born. I'd thought if I could still have the very same two children in my life without the way they'd gotten here, I'd choose that. I thought what an awful thing to want to hurt a person who wanted

to leave an unhealthy relationship. Then my thoughts shifted to
the one I was currently in and agreed that it too was unhealthy,
but at least I didn't have to face a judge to come to this conclusion,
and I had the power to change it. All of this was never about the
kids. It wasn't because I wasn't taking care of them. Nothing else
seemed to be working in the attempts to hurt me and if you want
to get the attention of a mother, you go through her children.

While still in the shower, I maneuvered my thoughts back to
my tropical waterfall that felt cool, soft as silk, like well water that
made your skin feel like a newborn baby. In there I felt safe and at
peace. I didn't want to leave this place. I needed to hold on to this
fantasy because no one had access to me in there. They couldn't
question me about anything, demand anything from me, or accuse
me of anything, and I was cool being alone in my surroundings
and with my thoughts.

I was ordered to bring the kids with me, but I wanted to leave
them behind and lie and say they had a thing or something that
couldn't permit them to come with me. I know that sounds crazy,
but drastic measures sometimes bring drastic ideas. Before this
day came, all my mind could see was: *Please make sure the children
are present for this hearing*. To me, it was saying, "Make sure you
bring those kids in case they needed to be handed over and be
prepared to drive back home by yourself!"

Here we go. While driving down the highway toward my
fate of possibly losing my children wore on me so thick that I
couldn't feel my clothes on me. My stomach was in knots and I
was completely numb. I drove for hours with this heavy on my
mind, but had to focus on being safe at the same time, and it was
tough. I kept looking at them both in the rear-view mirror and
praying to God that He wouldn't allow this. He saw how much
I worked at trying to keep things in order while trusting that it

would work itself out. Even though the judge stated it would be temporary if they had to go with their father, he was unaware of who I had been dealing with. Temporary was not on the agenda for the other party. Permanent pain was what the plans were toward me in any way possible without being incriminated. I felt this so strong and knew in my heart that unfortunately it wasn't exaggerated.

I just continued to pray while I drove, saying, "Lord, don't let this happen. Please." I even said to Him I knew I chose to do extra in my life that He hadn't orchestrated and was apologizing, and said I'd work on letting it go. I talked to Him throughout this drive and was praying He heard my heart and my words. I was a mess.

I was four hours away, still on my eight-hour route to home for court, when my cell phone rang. It was my job calling. Not only did my heart fall onto my sleeve, but my throat got all choked up and I was afraid of answering it. I just knew they were calling, saying they no longer needed me to come back to work because of obsessive absences. That they needed someone more reliable, even though they understood my situation. I couldn't handle another thing, so I hesitated, but still needed to answer so I would know what my next steps would be.

I answered slowly. "Hello?"

It was a lady from Human Resources. "Hi, Kimberly, this is Employment Services, and we were calling to offer you the job at our company and need to know if you would accept it."

Tears welled in my eyes now because immediately I was like, "Wait, what?"

She repeated herself and asked if I would accept and in that second, I broke down and had to pull over on the highway. I sobbed on the phone to this lady from Human Resources who had no idea of the whirlwind and hell I was going through and the oncoming defeat that I thought was getting ready to happen. She was taken aback by my tears and I hadn't answered yet, so I said, "Yes." I told her where I was on my way to and that she would never know, in a million lifetimes, what her offer meant to me.

She told me they had to mail the offer letter to me but needed my acceptance beforehand. At this moment, all bets were off with keeping my personal life personal and my professionalism, professional. I had to tell this stranger all that I was about to face so that she would get the picture of how huge this offer meant to me. I asked her, "In lieu of my situation, would you mind faxing the letter to the courts for me to let them know I had gotten the job permanently?" and she was more than happy to do so. She expressed her sympathy and prayers toward my situation and said to get her the number to fax the letter. I hung up and called the courts to get a fax number to the courtroom that my case was connected to and gave it to Human Resources.

After sitting there and praising God for His glory and love for me, crying out of joy for a change and not exhaustion, my children asked what was going on and I told them I'd gotten the job finally and things were getting ready to be just fine with us. I sat there for a moment to gather myself before getting back on the road and the rest of my ride was like a breath of fresh air. He heard me and knew my heart. He knew before I knew things were going to work out because He already had it orchestrated.

Out of all our getting, we are always to get an understanding. That was Word. I understood my fate was at hand and I needed Him to step in. I wasn't doing the right things; I wasn't reading my Word as I should and I was living in sin, trying to deal with chaos on top of chaos. I was calling myself a good person because

I was, but I wasn't always doing the right thing and despite that, He showed up for me. He spoke to me on one occasion and said, *If you stop chasing after him and chase after me, I'll give you the desires of your heart.* This was about the relationship I was currently in. I'll never forget that day that I thought all that was around me heard that voice, too, but hadn't. It's when I realized it was Him speaking to me. Even in this, I wasn't obedient, and He still loved me enough to step in and turn this around.

Arriving at the courthouse, I'd done what I was told and bought the children with me, along with my mother. Upon seeing their dad, they ran to him and the entourage of people, anxious to see what was thought to be my leaving without my kids. What they didn't know was who I had in my corner and that He didn't take too kindly to ill-intended hearts. They didn't know who I talked to in the middle of the night through my tears and trusted that He'd heard every word between sniffles, headaches from crying so long, and stuffed nose moments from being so knee-deep in prayer that I couldn't breathe. They would soon find out.

We went inside upon the Bailiff coming out to call our names and I'd told my attorney what had transpired while on the way here. Being that this was the only thing this court proceeding was about, I was the only one who had to take the stand to state my employment status. I could have floated to the stand in the air as happy as I was.

The opposing lawyer walked up to me in a very bold, aggressive, and confident manner and said, "Ma'am, we are here today to show the courts that your children need stability and are financially covered appropriately to flourish and maintain a healthy and well-provided lifestyle. The court needs to know if you have gained permanent employment yet?"

While the faces held smirks, I proudly stated, "Yes and my offer letter was faxed to the courts and should have arrived for the judge to see."

The judge smiled and was happy to oblige and stated that he indeed had received such a letter and was happy for me and even congratulated me upon my gained employment. Those smirks turned into disappointed looks as his whole entourage that came to gloat seemed to have deflated.

The judge said to me, "Are the children present?"

"Yes."

He then said that since there will be no need to award temporary sole custody to the non-custodial parent I needed to allow the children to spend some time with their family before leaving and that I was free to take them back home with no troubles or problems. He then stated to me, to the opposing lawyer, and his client, "Am I clear on this? You are to release them back to their mother upon her leaving for home." This was agreed. He also stated to the other party that a mockery had been made of his courtroom and he didn't want to see them there ever again.

Case closed.

God *is good!*

I celebrated with family and was all smiles and praises to my Father who made it all possible.

After all of this, the drive home went smooth sailing. We were all happy, and I was more than ready to move forward in everything. I was even ready to let go of all toxicity in my personal life so that my children and I could get back to our lives. The summer was coming up in a few months and I still had to honor our court order in meeting him at the halfway point. I can't say that I was looking forward to this as I needed a break from even the sight of the pain caused, and antics and the whole interventions of the courts.

The gap between the victorious win in court and summer was like a vacation to my mental mode. I no longer received a summons in the mail like a monthly bill, no more attorney attachments to read by email on either side, or having to see the smug looks. It was relaxing, and I pulled steam ahead. Anything after this was manageable because I'd won and still had my children.

Anger in things not going as planned grew. With all things attempted, I knew this wasn't completely over from the enraged look I received leaving the courthouse, which was creepy, and I felt it. I wanted so badly to say, "Let's just stop this and work through it as parents." I was happy that I was on the outside of that dark cloud and looking in. I saw clearly what I couldn't see while inside of it before.

Spring and summer ended up being about getting information from our children to twist their words around, manipulation, bribes with material things as usual, or plots on the next move against me. Even knowing things would not lay as they were, I wasn't sure what was in store. But it was over for right now and I focused on my new permanent job, the breather that I was given, and on putting my life back on track.

No matter what we face, God is in control. Sometimes when stuck in the middle of the sea, in a tiny little boat with no rafters to move to shore, all we have is that relationship and trust in Him. He will move the waters to ease us right onto shore unharmed. Stay encouraged to live. Live as though He has already anchored and taken care of your issues. This is how He'd want us to lean on Him, as if all we see is Him working while we are moving.

CHAPTER TWELVE

Why?

My breath of fresh air lasted for quite a while and I enjoyed every bit. Just as I'd gotten used to not receiving subpoenas in the mail and getting off work feeling happy to get the mail out of my box, I gazed upon a familiar-looking envelope. I thought, *Geesh, dude, give me and you a break already.* I didn't have a clue what this was over because things were over. I'd even thought that maybe this was something that got lost in the mail and arrived late. Things were normal again at home with the kids and me and hopefully, the time in between gave us both the time we needed to work through all that had happened. Not so.

It was like I walked around with a red circle in the middle of my forehead for a bull that would only receive satisfaction when he hit the bullseye with as much force as possible. Before seeing what was inside, I continued to pray it was a lapse in the postal service from previous deliveries.

Opening the envelope, it was a court order to appear in civil court in the state that I lived in and for the same reason I'd just gone to court for back at home. Turns out that since making a mockery of the first judge's house, someone thought he'd give it another go in a new state. No signs of anything positive like just enjoy our children and try to co-parent in sight. Just a conjuring up of the next move.

A rush of anxiety and a warm feeling came across me with anger. Why? It seemed like there was a constant plan, encouraged by a sinister soul, to take me out at every turn. I don't know. It was deplorably insane.

To have to prepare all over again for the same rodeo and mentally get ready to face yet another string of issues was more than appalling. Even though I didn't have to rent a car or take our children out of school, I still had to take time out of my life, off my job to obtain a local attorney that I couldn't afford and start this whole thing over again. The subpoena was to retry modifying custody, child support, my alleged substance abuse, and neglect of our children. *Are you kidding me!* Maybe he thought that since it was another state it would make a difference along with the added lies that visitation rights weren't allowed. (Maybe the definition of driving six hours to and from our meeting point was deemed as something else.) What was the volunteered given time for every school break with them called?

The accusations of this order were even more bizarre than the last time when I was apparently to be on drugs. It was literally written in the reasons for this one that the children were being neglected and mistreated by my getting mad at them for forgetting to take clothes out of the dryer and punishing them corporally or in a derogatory way. It also stated that our daughter allegedly said during one spring break visit that one time she volunteered to do a chore our son was supposed to do just so he wouldn't get brutally punished. It also stated that while visiting, our daughter said that she wasn't aware of how bad of an influence she was under while being with me and supposedly teared up while saying it. It stated that when asked how she felt during her visits, she said that she felt she could say what was on her mind without getting hit for it and being put down constantly. (Again, to this day, I have the letter she'd written about mistreatment during her summer visits along with the fake gift of a laptop that was bought for her birthday. She used it all while there, but then, when it was time for her to bring it back home, it mysteriously disappeared. She never saw it again.)

I asked my attorney why this was even allowed and was told that it was because of it being a different state but shouldn't be because it was for the same things. He'd stated that he would bring this up in court before the judge. It's called Concurrent Jurisdiction, where a person can choose to try someone in another state for the same thing if the judge allows the entry.

A co-worker referred my attorney . He was an older Jewish attorney who, upon meeting him, made me a little apprehensive because it just seemed to me he may have seen his days already as an attorney and possibly should retire. Resurfaced anxiety and stress crept back and the tears flowed again. That it was even researched to start this again was unbelievable. If you don't have the means to hire top-notch help in representing you, a game of Russian Roulette is at bay. The site www.lawyersofthesamepersonality. com had to have been sought again, and it was like I went to sleep and woke up feeling like the victory I'd won was just a dream because here we are again. The new opposing lawyer was not only like the last one from the other team, but you'd have thought that she'd been hypnotized or something. She looked at me as if I were a piece of trash that was out to take all that was available to take. I wasn't after anything but peace.

We went to court over the initial allegations and again, the person I was seeing was brought up and made the focal point in the whole thing. That seemed to be the reason more than anything else that was entered in the answers of why I was being taken back to court outside of the made-up things listed.

It was all so surreal, but here we are going through a repeated scene. I had to laugh to keep from screaming at the content in the order. No one had this type of money to waste or time over one person's misery. The lurking in the darkness because of whatever couldn't be released kept pulling at the heart and cheered the mind on to keep causing damage. Whenever I felt I had space to figure things out, a single track was removed to cause a collision.

There was nothing I felt I could do to put a stop to it. I kept facing an ongoing tornado that kept twisting and devouring everything in its path that wasn't bolted down. My body was limp from day to day and hidden from the world. It's amazing how we can lift and encourage others, but on the inside feel crushed and defeated. To look at me was to see this vibrant person with a huge smile behind a shattered heart and harassed life. Masks that had the days of the week on each of them, along with a description of what I needed the world to see over what was truly happening. The underlying person was dead mentally and physically. I was numb to this fight. I just wanted my happy.

In court I repeated the same steps as before by bringing forth my income, sitting on the stand to testify on my behalf, and brought up the issues of being able to hide behind the military as excuses as to why this thing couldn't be done or that. I bought up everything done under the radar with harassing me and this judge wasn't interested in any of it. So, I was at a loss and didn't know the purpose of my being there, if all that was going to be heard was the opposing party. I honestly felt as though this judge was already in favor of the military status and affiliation to the United States Government. My attorney wasn't really aggressively speaking on my behalf so I felt I had to defend myself so all I'd say was falling on death ears.

This time around, I didn't feel as confident in court. I was a little nervous; even though it was all bogus and full of deceit, because of the lack of funds for ample representation, the odds were against me. You get what you pay for. My health was fading, but I didn't have time to pay attention to it. I couldn't eat, my head hurt daily, and I'd had overwhelming things going on with my body that I couldn't control. There were times I pretended while talking to my mother long distance because I didn't need her to worry about me and my situation, that I'd make it appear I had a handle on things. I pretended to our children, reassuring them that all was going to be okay. I pretended to myself, playing out scenarios in my head how I could defend myself and get through this twinning of a case. I pretended to continue in a relationship I knew I should have ended long before any of this. My insecurities held on to it so that I could feel wanted and not thrown away, even though I was the only one who claimed that relationship. In my mind, I didn't realize I was being thrown away again because things were at least there when needed. Yeah, that sounds really crazy, but I'm about being honest and open to help someone else.

It was all so much that writing it now and rehashing it all is something I could never have believed one could endure had I'd not been the person who went through it. But I did.

I'd even wrote a letter to the judge explaining things of what I couldn't say in court, but it wasn't accepted because you can't write letters to judges. It was too much for my mental mode. I immediately realized the money given for representation did exactly nothing and I was fending for myself throughout this whole thing. Judge's only respect representation and really don't care to listen to the client.

Another visit from the circus came to town. With all the accusations, the case still couldn't prove me neglectful, on substance abuse and the child support or custody wasn't modified. Things settled back down and went back into its corner like a tiger retracting before attacking its prey just for a moment. Only for a moment. I'd seen enough courtrooms to last a lifetime, and I was over it. The judge ruled that there was no convincing evidence to prove me neglect and that things would convene after the children's summer trip away to see if we couldn't conclude the matter. He'd stated his awareness of this case being a repeated one, and it was time to put it to rest. This made me a little happy and a little uneasy, too. I couldn't really read this judge. I couldn't read his demeanor or body language at all. I got nothing from him but a cold shoulder because I kept speaking up while standing next to what should have retired long before this point, which was acting like an intern instead of a true attorney. So, I wasn't sure of the outcome of this round of hearings.

How many of you know that when one tornado touches down, there is another one somewhere starting to form from a thunderstorm with the winds being blown in different directions, spinning air near the ground that causes it to rise brewing up into another huge one? A whirlwind and the clouds start to get dark as if life-changing storms are on the radar, but you can't tell exactly when they will hit your side of town. This became my life.

Jesus was truly my strength in every inch of my weakness. I cried out to him while the kids slept. I wished I could've blinked twice and wake up from this nightmare and needed daylight to break through each dark paned window. How was it that the mistreatment I was receiving now worse than the reason I'd left? I needed all parties involved to sit down somewhere and be happy in moving forward.

While dealing with the fact that even after leaving and the divorce hadn't started good or was finalized, a whole marriage took place that our children participated in. Like all new women in a man's life, we tend to believe all that's said about the last woman, decide she can do "so much better" than the last one did and suddenly transform into Wonder Woman. Our children were already familiar with this situation as they were introduced on secretive outings even prior to my leaving.

School was officially out for the summer. I routinely packed up the children to go for their visit, and off we went for the exchange. When we arrived, saying goodbye to them this time, it was like handing them over for ransom or something. I felt chills this time and had no trust in this exchange, but had a court order to follow. I remember after getting back in my car, feeling bothered by this visit for some reason. God will always reveal things to us, but we won't get it if we aren't connected. We will simply say, "Something told me," when it's never something, but always either God or the enemy. Demeanors toward me were nothing short of distasteful and schematic. If I'd had my way, I would have turned back around with them still in the car and drove back home. Something was off. I regretted volunteering each spring and summer when the court only suggested every other spring and summer.

During their visit this time, I didn't intervene by calling them to say hello nor did they reach out to me. I hoped that the time spent would have gone peaceful and quality time would have interjected itself in place of past drama.

I prayed that the quality of treatment toward my daughter would be different from the times before. There were a lot of issues with treating her differently than my son. There was a lot of favoritism and clear mistreatment to the point of our daughter writing a letter about it expressing her feelings on how she'd be excluded from different things. I still have this letter. Before this visit, she'd been told that she'd gotten a laptop for her birthday and that she would get it the next time they came. When they went, she received it and could use it all the while they were there, but when it was time for them to come home and she wanted to bring it home with her, and it mysteriously came up missing and she couldn't find it. She called me and told me about it and I told her not to worry about it and to leave it where it was. Once she was gone, it mysteriously showed up during a conversation.

Similar things like this would happen to her while she visited, such as making her go to her room and sit in punishment over minor things that happened, and I couldn't understand why. It was clear of the differences that were being made between the two of them and I didn't even have to be there but heard in her voice over the phone. Communication between all adults involved wasn't possible. Believe me, I tried numerous times, but at the sound of my voice, venom would ensue. Unfortunately, nothing could be accomplished because of hatred. At least hatred is how I received it. It hurt because she needed me and I couldn't be there. Our son was happy-go-lucky as there was never a problem with him. He received any and everything he wanted. Talking to my son over the phone, he'd mention the things going on and I'd tell him to look out for his sister as much as he could.

However, they accused me of being unfit or neglectful. All I could do was shake my head at the thought of it all. I couldn't put my finger on it, but I knew that coming for me wasn't over and I never knew what was going to happen next.

When the time was approaching for school to begin and me to drive and meet six hours for the exchange, I'd gotten an unexpected call from my attorney while I was at work. He'd said that I needed to meet him at the Juvenile Court Division immediately. I thought to myself, *Okay, the children aren't here and*

I have no reason to be summoned to court because they were visiting already and we'd not spoken at all during this summer visit, argued or anything so what was this all about?

At a loss and no time to ask my attorney for an explanation, I had to ask to leave unexpectedly for an emergency court hearing that I couldn't even explain but was granted to do so. I even had to Google the Juvenile Court Division, being that I'd never been before, as it was a different courtroom. I can't even tell you the thoughts that raced through my head. I had no clue why I'd have to go to Juvenile Court when that was minor children, etc. I was clueless and my heart was racing and beating so fast that it sounded like drums for a finale that was getting ready to be announced.

I parked in the parking lot and while walking up the stairs I was flushed all over because this just couldn't be happening like court had become a magnet to me. As I walked through the doors and then through the metal detectors, putting my purse and keys on the belt, I looked up and saw my children standing on the other side of the detector. Immediately, I knew that this was the brewed storm that awaited me. This was that chill I felt when I took them to the meetup place for exchange. This was what God was revealing to me.

Happy to see my children and them happy to see me, we were walking toward each other when our meet was blocked as if they were being protected from me. That wasn't a really good move. I automatically went crazy and caused a huge scene to where the officer that was assigned to stand outside the courtrooms got in the middle and said, "What is going on?" I told him I was their mother and hadn't seen them all summer and the other party was nobody and that he'd better get them before I pop a head off like the cork in a wine bottle. He then stated to me to please not allow my children to see me act this way and that he'd hate to take the both of us into custody. He turned to the other party and said that they were my children and they needed to step aside. If I could spit fire from my mouth to burn off the head of a person, it would have been at that moment.

Still, I didn't quite know why we were there and what they had concocted up this time. The attorney I'd had stood next to me like before, as if he had already retired and just there to be moral support and speechless in defending me, so here I was again helpless. I've learned that judges are not so keen on hearing what the defendants have to say, especially when they have no representation. When there is representation, it is the only voice the judge will consider.

His attorney started by stating that we were there in attempts for her client to ask the courts for temporary custody as orders to Japan were received and was requesting that our children be able to go. She felt it would be in the children's best interest if they could experience such an opportunity and because the only time spent with them was during school breaks, more time was warranted. She said that her client wasn't comfortable leaving the states and having them stay behind with all they'd told him during their summer visit about things that were going on at home. It was felt that they were in grave danger and felt that they would be safer and were asking the court to grant this wish.

Instantaneously my neck got warm, my head started spinning, I couldn't feel the floor beneath me, I wasn't breathing and I couldn't see straight. I felt the tears wailing up, but I just could not go through the spell again and whine. I was ready for war. I was ready to jump over tables and lay hands-on people. I had enough. I wanted to lose all since of class, grace and all that I was made out of at that moment. It was the hardest thing in my life that I had ever had to do in controlling my emotions and my actions. Trying to keep it together without showing the anger that I'm sure they wished I'd shown the courts, I looked over at my attorney who had to be one of the worse in the state as he literally stood there scratching his head. (I wish I were making this up, but the truth is setting me free on more levels than you'll ever know.) Not saying a word, my attorney simply looked straight ahead and I said to him, "Are you going to say anything!?" I thought to myself, "This man had his attorney call an emergency court hearing without even consulting with my attorney or me and blindsided me! What the hell!" And this short, stubby, man with gray hairs coming out of everywhere who should never think about law again stood next to me didn't utter a word. I was livid.

Without waiting on him any longer, I took my chances and spoke up to plead my own case and said that as usual hiding behind the military was the crutch to obtain the one thing that this has been about from the beginning of taking me to court and that was to hurt me. I said that the interest in taking on the role of parenting wasn't it at all, but using the military as weight since nothing else has worked was always the option. The only thing known that would hurt me would be through our children, and I felt that it was unfair. I said that the entire time we've gone to court the main issue was the fact that I'd moved on in my life and was seeing someone and upon grilling our children and twisting every word they'd said, this was another attempt out of some sort of sickness to hurt me.

This judge blatantly disregarded all I'd said and suddenly, I no longer felt worthy. I stood feeling like some low class, incompetent, uneducated Black woman who had made bad decisions all of her life where our children were concerned and was exactly what he'd been successfully trying to prove in my being unfit. Looking at my attorney, my instincts were to knock him clean out, while picturing all of his paperwork he'd prepared for my case, that he never even once picked up to get involved during the court proceedings, fly all over the place. He stood there as if he was in awe or something and was in disbelief, but still never uttered a word.

All at once it was like time stood still and I'd gone off somewhere else. I was no longer in the courtroom mentally and had checked out. My body was experiencing this psychological breakdown. I felt lightheaded, and like I was floating. I was certainly there, but not there. I heard the judge say, "Let me speak to the children."

I looked over at the other party only to witness smug smirks on the faces of souls that did not worship or praise the same God I did and, in that moment, I wanted to go to prison at the opportunity of wiping the ugly sinister looks off those faces away. I wanted my suffering that they caused to have company. I was tired. I felt like I was in the boxing ring with endless rounds and no bell. The only thing I could think of was that killing me slowly was the objective.

Our son went back with the judge first and then our daughter. When the judge came back, he stated that upon speaking with the children, he was told by our son that he wanted to see what it was like going to Japan. He said he'd asked our son how he felt about my friend and was told the same thing he'd said years before that he liked him but missed it just being him, his sister and myself. At that moment, I felt guilty. I felt as though I was indeed unfit for allowing someone else to be a part of our lives and not separate my time between having a relationship and being a mother. All of a sudden I felt unfit. My heart broke at that moment and I crashed mentally.

Our daughter told the judge that she wanted to stay with me and that she wanted to finish school with her friends as she was in her sophomore year. The judge stated that she should have the right to do this. He'd asked her the same question about my friend and she'd stated the same thing as her brother. Again, the guilt was overwhelming. I had no idea.

What a lesson to learn and right there in court how unfortunate it was that one party could simply move on and live their best life while the custodial party had limits as to what they needed and wanted to do. I wasn't thinking; I didn't take the time out to weigh out my pros and cons when moving on. I beat myself up over that for a long time until God told me to forgive myself and move forward because He had. After being married for so many years to one person, then it ends and you go through the phases. You feel vulnerable, lonely and just want some normalcy for yourself. To feel needed and wanted again and no matter how the situation goes during the process, it appears it should be your right to go through it if that's your choice. I don't know. I was a mess.

This judge didn't make it any better because since the kids stated they missed it being just the three of us, he projected that toward me as if to confirm all I'd already felt in my guilt. Since my daughter wanted to stay with me, he ordered that our son get to go to Japan and our daughter could stay. He also ordered me to sever ties with this friend who was never summoned to court to speak up for himself. It was awful; no one had met him for him to have been deemed a threat. This was crazy, but I would do whatever I needed to do for my children. I was also ordered to allow their father to come to my home to allow our son to gather up some things that he may want to take to Japan with him. I stated no one was allowed inside my home and they would have to wait outside and the judge agreed.

I don't think I can explain all my feelings. I could never detail enough for you to understand what was going on in my mind, body, and soul. It seemed like a nightmare that I fought hard to wake up from. I was simply sick, hurt, in pain, and felt like the most hated person on the planet.

Temporary custody of our son was granted while being overseas as I had to approve this and sign permission for our son to get a passport. Our son was the youngest. He was my baby. My premature baby that I nursed to goal weight. We were always a package team. Our circle wasn't complete with one missing. One link gone enormously made an impact on things. On that day, I knew what it felt like to have your child taken from you. While I don't compare this to losing a child to death, but it sure felt that way to me, the agony was devastating. My heart shattered into a million pieces. My body was so tired from fighting a senseless fight. My mind was so drained that nothing made sense anymore.

The rulings, the nagging court appearances until he felt he'd won something over me, the missing hours at work, the bending backward and forward in driving six hours to meet for an exchange, the questions that I couldn't answer for my children because I didn't know the answers myself, the weary sleepless nights asking God, "Why?" was all just a blur.

I wasn't sure how I made it to the car. I cried so hard and felt so weak that a correction officer helped me outside. I still wasn't breathing regularly and couldn't believe what had just happened. The enemy kept pushing until the one thing that it was after, no matter how it ended, was accomplished. I gave birth to two children. How is it I am leaving with one and leaving the other one behind? What just happened? I remember getting in the car with my daughter and I couldn't speak, but was hysterical. I called my mother and at the sound of her voice I just sobbed and screamed in the phone, "Mama, they took my baby! They took my baby!" She had no idea what was going on because I hadn't had the time to call to tell her about this emergency hearing. I was past ill. I was past hurt. I was past anything that could have made sense of this whole thing. I was past it all. I looked at my daughter and said that I was sorry because I never knew how they felt about my having my friend become a part of our lives. If I'd known, it would have made a difference immediately.

I hugged her tightly for a long time and sat there because I couldn't drive right away.

It was around two o'clock in the afternoon when I'd arrived home. I remember the time because I waited for my son to come and take with him what he wanted to Japan. I remember the time because I kept looking at the clock, wishing it would just stand still. I wished somehow that it would rewind to when it was just the three of us traveling and on our way to our new lives in peace. I tried to piece some type of sense together as to what I was going to do and how I was going to say goodbye to my baby and not see him for two whole years. I know I agreed to allow him to go, but did I really have a say? It felt like the time on the clock was screaming reminders of how close it was getting to them arriving, and I wouldn't wish this feeling on anyone. Not even those who were going up against me.

They arrived and parked across the street from the house. Our son rode back from court with them and got out to come in, and I froze at the sight of him going to his room to pack. I wanted to talk him out of it and wished I could back out of the deal or anything that would make this whole ordeal go away. Our daughter went outside to see her father and talked with him while her brother got his things. My heart was beating fast and hurt like someone just sat on my chest for hours.

He'd gathered the things he wanted to take with him, which wasn't a lot, and said, "Mom, I have the things I want to take with me."

I looked him in his little handsome face and felt like I'd failed him and just held him for as long as I could. I told him how much I was going to miss him and how much I loved him but that we'd be able to talk and keep in touch. He cried and held on to me and I didn't want it to end. I watched my twelve-year-old, going on thirteen, son walk out of my life for longer than a summer vacation.

Even though I wanted to breakdown, I still had my daughter to consider, so I needed to hold it together as best I could for her. I had to make the changes the judge had ordered me to make to put pieces back together with my family, so I was severing ties with my friend. It was weird, however though because my daughter watched my every move like she was taking notes on how long it was going to take before he'd be leaving. He was to be gone within seven days. To be honest, I wasn't sad over it and wanted my family back in order.

A couple of days had gone by and I was just numb. I couldn't really sleep well and prayed more than I can even say for some answers to make things right and okay mentally. I couldn't crack up. This wasn't an option. I come from a very strong line of women and men and their blood ran throughout my veins, so I was built to survive even if I felt more like dying on the inside.

My son had gone, but communication continued between my daughter and the other party and more than usual it seemed. My spirit kept talking to me, telling me that something was still off. I didn't know what it was and couldn't put my finger on it, but my daughter was acting very unusual. She'd gone to school seemingly happy, but still kind of sad over her brother being gone.

I thought she was looking at this picture the same as I was with the circle being broken. I'd taken a few days off of work after this ordeal to sort through things and get my house in order, and so I took her out to eat to talk. While we talked, I assured her that our guest would leave and that we could get some normalcy in our lives. While talking to her, she looked like she wanted to burst with news that she hadn't shared with me. She had that look like, *I have something to say but don't know how to say it.* So, I asked her what was going on.

"Mom, I wanted to stay because I didn't want you to be alone but I want to go to Japan to experience being out of the United States, too, and be with my brother."

I felt my heart drop again . I hesitantly asked her what was in her heart because we always had honesty about feelings and I guess that's why I was so torn apart at them not telling me how they felt about my friend moving in. She said she didn't want to leave me but wanted to go overseas. I told her I was happy she didn't want to leave me but that she should have said this in court because now it was too late and they had gone already and we couldn't change things with the courts now. At that moment, I couldn't state to her all I'd felt because it was all too much for me to relay such feelings to a child. I needed my girlfriends. Someone I could really let go with.

The atmosphere somehow changed to it feeling like things were scripted or something but we'd just gone through a lot so I needed to keep it together and work my way through this. She said that she felt this way while talking with the Judge but didn't say it because she was worried about me. I assured her while silently I was going through a nervous breakdown that I was going to be okay and that my intentions were never to see us at this point where things seemed as though I'd disappointed the two of them. I assured her of how she and her brother were the two most important things in the world to me and that no one came before them. I felt the tears whaling up in my eyes and I was so tired of crying over everything at this point that I thanked God for holding them back so that I could speak clear enough.

What she said after this made my stomach flip and the food I'd just eaten suddenly was working its way back up my throat to where I had to swallow hard to keep it down.

She said, "Well, Mom, they aren't gone yet and are still here. If I changed my mind, they wouldn't leave right away, but I needed to make it up so they could check out of the hotel and get going." She was told that all would have to happen was to make the attorney aware and the judge would be informed of the change.

Hearing her speak was like all her words faded and all I could see was her lips moving. I drifted off into a whole other world, thinking all the way back to when she was first born, my son being born and how they turned into products for an adult instead of human beings. How the enemy is so dark that he would say or do anything and make it look like good intentions for us but the hidden agenda has nothing at all to do with a good heart. I really didn't know what to do with my feelings anymore.

I'd told her that if she really wanted to, I'd let her and tried my best not to show the hurt or disappointment in my face. I said that I wouldn't stand in her way at experiencing something that most kids wouldn't have the chance at. I called my half assisting attorney to report this change, and he noted that I'd have to come to his office to sign another paper giving permission for another passport and he'd notify the courts. In a day, I had to go through the whole goodbye scene again.

Again, I took time off work. I went to sign the papers, feeling knots in my stomach accompanied with the scene I knew I had to face all over again. The car being parked across the street, my daughter packing what she wanted to take with her and me watching the clock. My son ran into the house to hug me again with tears in his eyes. I reassured him it was okay and how much I was going to miss the two of them, but that we could stay in touch. Inside, I was reassuring something that I wasn't confident in and was trying to reassure myself of the same. It felt like being in a haunted house where you are walking down the corridors knowing that at any moment something is going to jump out at you and you try embracing yourself, but when it does, you are still scared and surprised. It still causes your heart to beat at a rapid pace and you try to gather yourself. We all embraced one another in tears and it was time for them to go. I watched them walk out and away. Not only one of my babies, but both. I thought at that moment how God must have this plan that was a far off one because how could I be going through so much pain, maintain and stand strong enough to make it through this. What could He possibly want me to get out of this?

The house I'd lived in had a huge picture window that you could see out but no one could see in. The kids were already settled in the car as I watched, waiting for them to drive off. Instead, one person got out of the car and walked back to the trunk, all the while staring at my front door like they were waiting for me to come out. I'd already decided that I would not give any more satisfaction at even seeing me at all. It was acted upon as though the bags in the trunk had to be situated, but all the while faces still looked toward my front door. The other party got out of the car to walk back there and suddenly the adjusting stopped. They walked slowly to get back in the car. As if they could see me watching, a smug smirk crossed their faces and waves as if to say, "Aha, now I have your children." Yes, this is when I wanted to give up what was wished for and go outside and take all my anger out on the situation for being so tacky and classless, but I thought of my children. They drove off and my body went limp.

I was slipping into a deep depression. I wept harder, watching the car pull off. Twisted like red tape, I collapsed as my friend tried consoling me. I'd tired of venting to my friends and family about my issue, so I started talking to my depression. I even allowed it to talk back to me, constantly reminding me of all of my unhealed scars. I was told that because of all I'd gone through, I'd start being taken on trips and doing things together and it would make time go by. This never happened. On one hand, he was there for me at times and with the other hand it was like an emotional and mental slap in the face. I was an injured bird with one wing broken and with the lie that we'd be okay and wasn't, broke the other wing again. I was alone most times. The brokenness in me and neediness in me stayed in a one-sided relationship. I felt that now they're both gone he didn't have to leave now and truth was it wasn't because I was slow or dumb. I didn't want to be alone. Crazy, huh? I didn't want to be alone, but was alone.

CHAPTER THIRTEEN

Lessons Come in All Shapes and Sizes

It felt like I was under attack, left with no weapons to fight. All this time, I didn't know my weapons were working. I just couldn't see them. I saw disappointment, regret, and pain. Day after day, I was in limbo, as if I no longer belonged anywhere.

Attending a church I grew to love, as I sought God, my pain was revealed. I was lost. I knew Him and believed He died on the cross for me and rose again, but I didn't *know* Him. The lady that helped me get my job was the one who invited me to this church where she was also a member.

Going to church and hearing a great Word, I allowed the *taught* Word to resonate in my heart. I needed another perspective besides my own and my friends telling me what they would do if it were them. I sought understanding of how I got to this point of not having my children and being in the wilderness alone. The blinders were on because my feelings and trauma were all I saw, but I became thirsty for healing. It was all I had left.

God sends what you need when He knows you need it, and not when you feel you need it. He sent someone who would reveal my truths to me. I'd gotten close to an elderly lady in the church, and one day, she had broken down all I'd had inside. Telling her

144

gave me a release and even though it was embarrassing and I had laid all my dignity on the line, it could not have been worse than keeping it all in and walking like a zombie day in and day out.

She gave me truths about my actions and she understood my pain. First, I had to deal with the harsh realities made by my own hands to start my healing process. It was longer than I imagined I'd bear.

"Baby, you livin' in sin and comin' to church like you got it all together, raising your hands and praising God, giving Him thanks. Whatchu thankin' Him for?"

I looked at her sideways, like someone confused by a simple question. I had no words, but she had plenty left to say.

"It's time for you to walk away from the situation you are currently in. It's time to get out from under that environment and face all you need to face without distraction."

I'd made excuses, tried to convince her it was a living agreement for financial purposes. I'd told her we had our own separate rooms.

"Baby, Mama wasn't just born yesterday, don't give me that. You may have two different rooms, but that don't mean you sleeping separately. I want you to look for your own place. Don't you know God shall provide all of your needs and He don't want you depending on no other man but Him? Don't keep coming up in here, sitting next to me, thanking Him, and then leave to continue living that way because you are better than that and He wants better for you."

All I could say was, "Yes ma'am." This, and constantly hearing the Word, kept weighing heavy on my heart. Very soon after that, I moved out and into my own.

"Lord, what did I do? How did I let things get like this and to this point?" I did what I needed to do to start this healing process and even though my heart and mind were on the same team, my flesh was on another. I'll never say I was on fire for the Lord so much that I was just that strong to resist and simply move on. I wasn't. I took many baby steps because at least one month had passed and I hadn't heard from my babies. I attempted to call them both and what started out going straight to voicemail turned into *this number is no longer in service.* I'd researched other means of how I could get in touch with them and it failed.

One stipulation of the court was that I was to have communication with my kids. Like all other court orders that I never initiated, he never followed the rules. It didn't take long for me to realize that all communication between me and the children had been purposely cut off. I didn't know what part of Japan they'd gone to. I did not know when they left the United States, when they arrived overseas, nothing.

While we were in court, and because of poor representation, I couldn't ask for the destination information to know where they would be. I only knew the bare minimum as far as the city and state. I didn't know which military base, future address, or anything. They both no longer had their Facebook accounts, which had been closed down. Both Instagram accounts had been suspended as well. I had nothing to go on.

As I laid down at night in my place that I'd moved in alone, it was more than my being alone. It felt like death. I can't blame all I was going through on a person I chose. I couldn't blame all I was going through on the choices made and done toward me while in this situation. I connected with someone who God did not plan for me. Even so, it was the only intimate thing that would temporarily relieve I felt would ease my flesh of the pain it felt. Even though I was still trying to heal from the masses of all we'd dealt with between us, my trials and tribulations, still going to church faithfully, my children and all that was transpiring in my life, I still chose to satisfy my flesh because this was what I thought I needed. It changed nothing; it didn't turn things around relationally nor did it bring me closer to any breakthroughs. Continuing this my way made things worse. I expected a knight in shining armor that was supposed to place a blanket over my chaotic turn of events. I unfairly expected the miracle to come through a person instead of being patient and waiting to hear from God and the rightful steps needed to get through.

I made a mistake by moving in a man amongst my family that was fragile and I didn't see it. The only fragility I saw was my thinking that I had this right to do this to help myself get by and felt I owned this right. I entered a war that I wasn't quite ready for because of my wanting to move forward with my life. I'd made a misstep.

I couldn't repair the broken pieces of my own, let alone someone else's. Instead of sweeping my pieces into the trash, I held onto them because that's where I was mentally. It helped for a couple of months, but after a while, it no longer cradled me enough to feel remotely normal. I realized that I'd just allowed what I'd walked away from to lay beside me, only to see that I was walking backward and my move became in vain. Without my children, my purpose was void. I had no reason to be here any longer. Not hearing from them, pretending to be loved by what wasn't love at all, and going to work like all was fine, had me spiraling out of control, to a point that once I said no more to temporary fixes bought on depression I'd never experienced before in my life. It grew so much that I wanted to leave this world. The darkest of darkness was the only way to describe my life.

Thoughts of suicide visited me daily. Satan kept saying things to me like, "What's the use? Your children are gone now, and you allowed it to happen, so why stick around?" He said it was my fault and that I knew how the heart of my adversary was toward me for having the nerve to leave and I'd given him what was needed to carry out things and since I had, the connection between my children and me was gone forever. He said I let a man come before my kids and even though it wasn't the mother in me or my character, I let my judgment get in the way and that they were now disappointed in me and wouldn't ever forgive me. He made all my praises in church feel like I was simply miming, but wasn't there in the presence of God. All I could see and focus on was the darkness I was in. The enemy constantly reminded me by the surrounding silence that I was alone now and I would never lay eyes on my children again since I let them go overseas. He spoke to my heart, telling me I thought I was signing permission to give my children a chance at experiencing one thing, but it was really my signing them away from me for life. I felt as though my life had finished and nothing else mattered to me. I didn't care anymore about anything.

At work, I smiled, dressed the part, and did my job, laughed at jokes, participated in pitch-ins, all while dying inside. Inside, I wanted to scream but didn't have time to do it or it would've taken too long to switch back into professional mode. Different ways how I would end my life started creeping in so much that I could see myself in the act.

The harder I tried holding on for my children, the louder the voices got for me to end it. I missed them. I needed to hear their voices. Days went by where the only conversation I had was with the television. It was work, home, sleep, church, and sleep again, not necessarily in that order all the time. I tried to instant message my son only to receive a message saying, "This person no longer wishes to receive messages." That crushed my heart, and I cried daily.

Days turned into months with still no sign of life or contact. I kept thinking about things like my daughter's upkeep with her eczema or how the new climate may affect my son's asthma, the schools they attended, what was going on in their daily lives, or the friends they'd met.

I kept going over and over in my head the scenes of signing papers and agreeing to them going, saying goodbye to them, seeing them sheepishly wave at me while driving off with my children, the court scenes and orders, the fact that it was known that the only way I could truly be hurt was through my children and things didn't stop until that was succeeded. I was more than a mess and cried myself to sleep nightly. Sometimes I'd wake up shocked that I woke up and at times wishing I hadn't. God was sitting with me and walking with me and I never saw the company.

One Sunday, as usual, my second mother, who God blessed me with, told me it was time for me to fight and start talking back to the devil.

"Baby, it's time to stop crying and stop waddling in the mess and do something about it. You don't have any more time to keep crying over spilled milk. They are still your children. God didn't allow things for you to hide and He didn't allow this to hurt you, but for you to see you. He gave those children to you, so fight."

I held on to her words for strength, like hanging on the very edge of a cliff, praying not to fall.

Every chance she got, she spoke into my life, telling me where I was wrong in wanting my situation to change without changing myself. She'd pray with me over the phone. I received a small slither of hope through her prayers but suddenly realized that when she wasn't around, room for the enemy was still there to keep messing with my mind regarding my children and my situation.

No more crying. I started researching my options of how I could contact my children. I'd called the American Embassy overseas and was told that I'd have to contact the Command for whereabouts. Their purposes only focused on residents who currently lived in Japan that may want to migrate to the United States or the issuances of visas to Japanese Nationals and legal residents of Japan. Because of failed attempts in the past with Command, I was apprehensive about this. Besides this, I didn't know who to reach out to because I didn't know any information to give to get to the Command they were attached to. So, I wrote letters in my free time to the list of Commanding Officers in the D.C. area that showed up as I surfed the Internet, looking for anything military-based, and copied these same letters to the Director of the White House Military Office.

I'd even started reaching out to different celebrities like Steve Harvey and his wife, Marjorie, that I knew helped individuals out in different cases. I felt if they could only hear my cry for help through social media like Twitter, Instagram, or Facebook, that my message out of a million would somehow seep through the cracks and get to them. I'd sent a letter to Oprah Winfrey and mailed it to Harpo Studios, thinking, *I don't know if they would even recognize this letter from little ole me.* I knew this was a long shot because they received letters, messages, etc. daily and all I could do was pray that somehow my letter or post would get through. It didn't. My letters to D.C. turned out unsuccessful. This was crazy, but I kept trying to reach out to people of prominence such as Tyler Perry, and went on his social media page and wrote to him, trying to get someone, anyone, to help me with my situation.

Praying for a breakthrough became my daily routine. My prayers became pleas to Jesus to give me anything, as I was just desperate to know they were okay at this point. I needed something. I was grasping at straws that weren't giving me a return. One day as I was walking out of Walmart, I ran into my son's best friend's grandmother, who asked me about the kids as she knew my story as well with our relationship through my son and her grandson. Before I knew it, I teared up and told her I'd not talked to them since they left and all that I'd tried to do to access any communication with them.

She looked at me and said, "Well, I can tell you that my grandson and your son play together on Xbox and talk to each other on there and your son cried and told my grandson that he wanted to talk to you and couldn't." She said he wanted to know if I was still in the same place and how I was doing. He was venting to his friend all along, according to her grandson, about how things were and some things that had been going on since they'd made it overseas. She stated that she'd talked to him through the game and told him she was sure I was okay and that if she saw me, she'd let me know he was concerned about me.

She also said before we parted ways, "Trust me, whatever is going on, it's not a bed of roses and your son is unhappy."

While I was working, God was, too. The information I received wasn't expected, but it was a part of the breakthrough I needed to at least know that there was still life. It broke my heart not to be there for my son and getting just that bit I got from her meant everything to me. I suddenly recognized that this situation would not work through my doing, but God's. I learned the hard way that I had to go through this and it had to play out His way and not mine. My hands kept working in it though. Even when I knew I didn't have power like Him, I somehow still felt like there was just a little more I could do to get what I want right away. Not so.

Of course, I didn't have Xbox and if I did, I wouldn't have had the slightest idea how to operate it. The words she'd spoken to me stuck in my head for days. Not only knowing that my son was worried about me, I was worried about them, too.

I consistently tried contacting both of my children through Instagram. Even though they weren't activated, I would still send random messages hoping they'd reactivated their accounts. I sent messages to them both daily with no responses. Finally, one day my son, who was going on thirteen, answered one of my messages. HALLELUJAH! I think at the sight of his message, I was speechless and overwhelmed with happiness. I immediately teared up as his message said, *Hi, Mom. I miss you.* I'd written back and typing didn't seem fast enough for all I'd wanted to say. I asked him about his sister and what happened to their cell phones, how much I missed them, and wanted to talk to them. He said that their Internet pages were shut down and cell phones were turned off from being told that they wouldn't need them overseas. At this point, this wasn't my focus, as I was happy to be talking to my son. I told him how important it was to talk to them and to get up to speed on how things were. We tried figuring out what to do to communicate, and he told me he'd think of something, but he couldn't stay on the post and needed to get off. As much as I didn't want to let go, I knew he had to go because of the circumstance. Even though I was sitting there thinking, *What? I'm his mother. Really?* I understood and hesitantly had to say goodbye. My heart, however, was glad and it was what kept me breathing longer more than not wanting to breathe at all. I was given a breakthrough.

I held onto that conversation for dear life with images in my head of what could be going on and how things were for my daughter.

This would be the first and last conversation I'd have with my son while months came about with no sign of contact. Suddenly, the message access disappeared, and it was like he'd vanished into thin air.

I lost sight of reality because I'd stayed too long on focusing on my own personal needs. I'm woman enough to admit it. The things I wanted, the things I felt entitled to, the things I thought wouldn't affect anyone because it was something personal, I was orchestrating. This is so far from the truth. I tried to have it both ways by having a route of escape from my personal trauma and continue to mother all at once. This wasn't God's plan or will for me. Losing sight of things out of my pain and watching that very thing bite me through the court system was simply too devastating to handle. I guess that's why I was so hard on myself. I pride myself from day one of motherhood to be the best mother there could be for my children and at this moment, I felt like a complete failure. I've learned that all pain, although tormenting at times, isn't bad pain but necessary nonetheless.

Again, many thoughts kept coming fast from Satan upon not knowing if I'd ever have that chance again at hearing my children's voices. Not knowing if I'd ever get to read another message was like meat dangling in front of a hungry lion. Not knowing what I would do to myself to no longer feel this pain, I had to make a choice, and I'd started applying for jobs back home. It was time to get closer to my livelihood, my family and friends, and new air. Within a few days of doing phone interviews on my lunch hours, I'd gotten a job offer to work once I went back home. This was God orchestrating the start of my healing process. I'd called my mother and told her I needed to come back home. I told her that if I'd stayed another week that I wouldn't make it. She told me she didn't care what I needed to leave behind. I needed to get on the highway and do just that. Come home.

This was my darkest hour. I'd always wondered what or how could a person want to take their own life. Relating to a situation will always be the best understanding of what may or may not make sense in making decisions. Had I not gone through what I had, the thoughts of taking my own life would never have crossed my mind. At that point, whether rich, poor, sick, or indifferent, you are not exempt from being human with unstable emotions. I wasn't any better or worse than anyone else. I needed God to step in and in a mighty way. He gave me the out to move forward to continue living. He wasn't ready for me and had I chosen to take this route, I would have sealed my fate and would not have been given the chance at heaven. There is a light at the end of the tunnel and the time frame to seeing it may seem far off but hold on because it's there.

I got on the highway and headed home. The best decision I could have made for my life, which depended on it.

CHAPTER FOURTEEN

Connected

It was a while before I'd heard anything else from either of my children. I wasn't okay, but being near friends and family made all the difference in the world. I was back home, trying to find myself again, after leaving a toxic marriage. Seeing the insides of courtrooms, learning the hearts of man and the length he would go for detrimental purposes was a chore. However, I was on the right track in locating who I used to be. I was doing okay with being a single mother, nurturing and teaching my children the things they needed to know for them to be successful with caring hearts. In mothering them, I did nothing wrong and that truth will never change.

Signing those papers, permitting the kids to go overseas, felt as though I'd signed a paper in blood to the devil himself. Later, I was told that if I'd had a decent attorney, I would have known that I didn't have to sign, and had they'd taken them overseas anyway, it would have been a kidnapping charge instead, no matter what the judge ruled. Well, I didn't know, and I felt I was doing the right thing, as I needed them to see how it was living with each parent. I wanted the experience for them to be great. Not one ounce of me suspected premeditated wrong intentions. Revisiting things was like clockwork in my head daily. Trying to make sense of it all, needing to breathe, and getting a closer relationship with God was my focus.

Arriving home and in time finding my own place was again in silence but this time I could breathe better because I was within driving distance of an outlet if I needed it. I was only a couple of hours from my mother and everyone else, so I didn't feel so alienated from familiarity.

And so, it begins working through what I had no idea was going to work with my not being in contact with my children.

I remember walking around in the empty house I'd found and saying, "Okay, Lord, I'm here now. What do you want me to do?" As soft as silk and as clear as a bell, I heard, *Build a relationship with me.* I broke down in tears, mentally exhausted from trying to hold it all together. I was able to let it all out. Inside, I was scared and had no other choice but to work on surrendering all I'd tried to control on my own. It hurt so badly. How could this be happening to me? I loved my children so much, just as any mother would, and I didn't deserve this. I remained resentful and unforgiving with bitterness in my heart toward the smug smirks and looks each time the thought of *Yeah, I finally got revenge* played in my head. Wanting to be okay was a stretch. I heard Him speak and was hesitant only because of my mental state, but was ready to build my relationship with Him.

God was ordering my steps, as all things were falling into place, one by one—receiving employment before I arrived back at home in Indiana, finding my new place, and being a work in progress openly was at bay and even though inside I hurt, I was okay and felt safe. Anyone who has children, at the thought of being cut off from them with no control over it, can only imagine my pain. It is unexplainable and will never be, no matter how long it becomes a part of the history of any journey.

I'd found a church through an invitation and eventually joined. I missed serving and missed being in the presence of God along with receiving the good Word. There is a difference between getting a goosebump and shouting over receiving a revelation in your life. This is what I needed. I studied and prayed. I met some beautiful people at my job and things were getting a little better. I now had an outlet I needed to deal with things.

One day I tried to reach out to my children again on Instagram, since that was the way I did it before. I'd sent both the same message, telling them how much I missed them and I asked them to forgive me for any pain I may have caused them over this whole situation. I needed them to know that I had not given up on trying to stay in communication with them and how much I loved them. Days went by with no response, but while I was at work one day, I got a message from my son telling me we could talk through Talkatone, a free app that gives free numbers for people to use to call and text free, as long as you have Internet connection. He told me to download the app, and he would give me a number to call so we could talk. *Man!* I couldn't wait to get off work and attempt it. I don't think my face was big enough to hold the smile that plastered across it. I couldn't wait to hear their voices. Since the time difference between the United States and Japan was, literally, night and day, he told me when to call.

I remember staying up late just to make this call and when my son answered; hearing his voice made me tear up instantly, and I wanted to jump through the phone. He told me he missed me and that his sister was going through a lot of things; she wasn't being treated right. He said they've got phones but weren't allowed to give the numbers to anyone, not even me. Also, their passwords weren't private, to keep up with what they were doing. This broke my heart, but I couldn't waste this call focusing on negativity.

"What do you think of Japan?"

"I like it, and I have some cool friends, but the schools are harder. I'm still making A's in my classes."

We talked about how the buildings there looked different and were shaped compared to the buildings in the United States.

"I'm proud of how you're keeping up with your grades. Tell your sister I love her and can't wait to talk to her, too." She'd gotten a job and was working, so I wasn't able to talk to her.

Even though I was afraid to hang up—I didn't know if we were going to talk again—he had to go.

"Nobody knows about this app, so no one knows that we've talked," he said, which was good to hear. He told me he and his sister were going to call me again or I could call him at the same time. We said our goodbyes and I just wept.

Though my heart was bursting with joy after hearing his voice and knowing I had a connection with my son, I still felt like the toxicity my children were being shielded from, completely alienated me out of their lives. While unfortunate my children had to come up with a way to communicate with their mother, I was elated they were smart enough to do so. However, I still cried myself to sleep that night. What mother wants to be on a planned calling schedule with their children? I was willing to accept anything I could get, as some communication was better than none.

Missing my kids was like missing the air flowing through your airway when you choke and you know you can't make it without it. I don't even know if that was a good enough example of how I felt.

Hearing my son's voice gave me strength. Hearing the Word made me more confident and my faith grew with truths and accountabilities that hurt but were necessary to own up to. Clarity on things crept in day by day. My truths were excruciatingly painful when I looked back through my life, through my marriage, my relationship, my real perspectives on who I was as a person versus who I was trying to be, which caused more pain. It was after the fact that I saw what I should've done over what I did. Facing my truths connected me to a better me. Many nights God revealed truths I'd denied, and that I fought with Him on, trying to make justifications, but He wasn't having it. It was all or nothing to heal, and no matter how long it was going to take, He was going to see to it I made it through.

I had a long way to go to completion, but I was still here despite all the enemy tried to do to break me. I was still here.

Each time I got through on this app with my son, I could only talk to him and not my daughter. This concerned me, but didn't want to put this on my son, so I asked him how she was doing.

"She's found some friends and is working all the time. Her bed was taken out of her room so she has to sleep on the floor."

"Why?"

"Because she wasn't keeping her room clean."

He told me he would wake her in the morning, when they weren't there, to let her sleep in his bed. My heart broke.

"Tell her I really want to talk to her."

"Because they didn't know about the app, the only time we can talk, she's at work."

In the evenings, everyone was home so it was hard to talk to her. I was worried because now I needed to at least hear her voice. You know when you hear your children's voices it always says everything you need to know about how they are because you gave birth to them and know them through and through. I know what every tone and facial expression means. I wasn't there. I couldn't see the whole scene of things. It sucked to not give words of encouragement or mother my daughter at all from where I was standing.

"It will get better and you have to come home soon enough. I can't wait to see you! I'm proud of how you're looking out for your sister. Keeping on doing it, son."

We could only spend a small window of time on the phone, but it was like heaven to me. It was what I held onto, like life support.

Continuing to reach out to my daughter on Instagram, wanting to tell her how I felt about missing her and that I wished I could be there for her when she needed me, failed. I started thinking that maybe she was resenting me or didn't want to talk to me. I didn't know what to think. I scanned her page daily for recent posts and there was nothing until I finally saw her page open and a video that she'd put together on her Instagram page, which was three parts to it.

What I saw crushed my spirit. The person I saw wasn't the daughter I knew, and it killed everything inside of me. The person I saw was broken, dark, and seemed to be alone in an unknown world. I was devastated.

The video, which I still have saved on my phone to this day, was about the treatment she was receiving. Her appearance was one that I'd never seen, so besides her words, I couldn't get past that. She always had beautiful hair, curly like mine, and was natural. I'd told her not to allow anyone to put any heat on her hair or chemicals in it, but despite what I said, her hair was damaged and ruined. She'd had it straightened and it was broken off in spots and unhealthy. She never wore all the makeup that she now wore and her entire demeanor was off. Hearing her rant and vent matched her appearance, and it took a lot of life out of me. I saw my daughter emotionally abused and scarred. There was nothing I could do. She never responded to my message about the video. Again, I assumed she resented me.

On her day off, I finally got to talk to my daughter. I told her how much I loved her and wanted to be there for her. She played things off as though it was okay and she was okay, like nothing was going on. She said that she worked a lot and had school and that she'd met some cool friends. I didn't push things and played along because of our limited time on the phone. I was happy I had the opportunity to tell her I loved her and wished I was there for her whenever she needed her mom, but to feel my hugging her when she needed a hug. I reminded her to believe she was worthy of all the things God had for her. I tried building her up as much as I could with that phone call. I asked about her hair to see what she was going to say and she said, "I know, Mom. It broke off but I'm going to start all over and it will grow back." When I told her the hair products to get, she said the products were very expensive there as opposed to how much the products made in China were in the United States. I said that I could send her some but needed the address. Of course, she couldn't give it to me.

I didn't make a big deal out of that with her because the time given was too precious to waste. I told her what to do with her hair to start over and to never get it straightened again. I reminded her that no one can make you do what you don't want to be done to your personal being and that her hair didn't need the excess heat. I was just happy talking to her and told her I couldn't wait to see them again.

My mental calmed down after being able to hear my daughter's voice. I felt I could finally keep in communication with them through Talkatone. It didn't last long, however. Immediately after my communication with my daughter, my son wasn't calling anymore. I kept calling through the app but got no answer. It made me nervous. It was the only lifeline I had to either of them. My son's number was no longer in use. Back to the drawing board. I started sending messages again, but this time I received no more responses.

Right then, the only thing keeping me from hurting myself and not wanting to be here on this Earth was God. He allowed the connection between me and my children because He knew I needed it and so did they. I was close to home now, which showered more hope into my life. Those thoughts didn't disappear right away, but eventually faded away during my willingness to heal. He gave me what I needed to get to the next level. Our conversing with each other lasted approximately three weeks and before it was over, I spoke with my daughter and for that, I will forever be grateful.

The confirmation of things being shut down between the kids was clear so there I was again in this headspace. I had made the first step, which was to remove myself from the memories in one place that surrounded me and haunted me and moved home. From there, I kept putting one foot forward and walking toward whatever was going to be my better days.

Upon walking away from everything to heal and to find peace during my tornadoes, I turned back to a piece of that storm while praying that God would fix things and heal my wounds. I went back to territories that caused some of those wounds. I'd made excuses why it wasn't so bad that I wanted to see my friend again because he wasn't a bad person. He was where he chose to be in his life. I knew it was too much for me to deal with, but I held onto our history, dating back to high school. The familiarity. I left it when I left to come back home, but he kept coming home to visit and wanted to visit with me. I allowed it.

I opened the door and let it in once again. I had a soul tie to it. He'd come into town, visit and stay with me, lay with me, and leave. It's what I wanted at the time. It was a numbing mechanism. I needed to numb the pain. He was the next best thing to filling a void for me.

He was and is a beautiful person who has a wonderful spirit but was flawed just as we all are in our own brokenness. We connected at the wrong time in our lives, unhealed from past things or just simply being who we were. I started things in the very beginning, thinking I was ready to move on.

Things lasted for a little while until God and the Word I kept receiving stepped in boldly and made me realize I couldn't walk away to heal from what I wouldn't let go of or all that was ailing me. It was time to let go, and it was hard. It was a hard soul tie that I wanted to change into what I felt he needed to be for me. He wasn't looking for what I needed and to be honest, I didn't need what I thought I needed from him. I was depending on someone who couldn't provide what I needed. I needed Jesus. I needed me to get to know me.

The next time my visitor came in town, and before our predictable actions of what made it feel like it was a relationship, the Holy Spirit spoke to me. When I was about to continue numbing my needs, He said, *No more! It's time to face things and heal!* It was like a tug of spiritual war. My heart and mind knew it was time, but my flesh didn't agree, so I stopped before it started. "Please, don't do this," I told him. "I can't do this anymore and if you've ever loved me, you won't continue to try." He was not an aggressive person so he listened. That was the last time I compromised God's will for my healing.

I surrendered to the Holy Spirit; I was losing a battle I could no longer win. I'd felt like a failure in motherhood, as a wife, and now my worth was in question on just maintaining a regular relationship and the worth wasn't enough to make him want to only commit to me because it was my job to count my worth and not his. I was a mess. A hot mess. It wasn't a regular relationship. It wasn't a relationship at all. I faced it and ended things physically and tried to maintain the friendship, and we did.

Having gone through the things I went through in the relationship showed me a different me. It showed me how I managed my womanhood and compromised it. It showed me the strength I didn't know I had. It showed me pain I didn't know I could overcome while overcoming added pain. It showed me the possibilities of growth spurts from a simple flashback that made comparisons to my actions then and what my actions now would be. It showed me that even though it's been a long time since I've been in a relationship, when it's time, I will know how love looks and what love feels like. Love never lies, no matter what package it comes in. I've learned that in adulthood, love is just like in childhood, where a child knows where true love is coming from just by paying attention to what's being given and shown. In adulthood, we maneuver things to make it look and feel how we need it to, and this is a false sense of love that is not of God.

No more blaming others for my chosen soul ties. I chose to marry without confirmation, counseling, or God's endorsement. I chose to be tied up to another familiar soul that wasn't waiting for me to bind up. I found it, and out of vulnerability, loneliness, and feeling as though I had every right after waiting a long time to move forward to date again, added it to my world. I chose to be bound to it, good or bad. It was my choice. I know it's easy to place blame so that we can take the burden and weight off us, but accountability is real and cheating on the truth is fake.

The Word says that when we don't wait on God and heal from the last situation, we are empty. All that happened before may seem over, but because we don't fill ourselves up with Him and wait, but choose to move forward on our own, not only does Satan come back, but he brings seven more spirits with him. We end up worse off than before. (Mathew 12:43-45)

I needed to heal and find a place to put all the choices I'd made.

Fresh off the press now that it's me, myself, and I, no more in and out of relationships, no more communication with my children, no more blaming anyone. It's just me. Suicide was no longer an option and off the table.

I needed my children. That's all I wanted. Temporarily, the enemy had a victory. Hurting me was finally executed and hurt my soul, it did BUT God.

Going to church, paying my tithes, studying the Word, serving in church, working, hanging out with friends from work and from home sometimes, being able to drive a small distance to visit family, and shopping became my things to do. It was just what the Father ordered, and I enjoyed the break.

Repetitively listening to sermons from Sarah Jakes Roberts, John Jenkins, Michael Todd, and T. D. Jakes, to name a few, for continued strength, was more than helpful. They got me through some rough days and nights when I felt like breaking over feeling isolated. I was building my relationship with Christ and had to change my perspective on being in a relationship with me.

Two years had come about and I hadn't heard from my children. I was at work when I received a call from my daughter. The call was noticeably clear, and it wasn't an overseas telephone number. She told me they were back in the United States and immediately I said, "I'm coming to see you guys." My whole body lit up on the inside like a Christmas tree.

I told my supervisor what had just taken place. It's sad that after going through so much, I felt obligated to let management know a little about my life just in case something else happened. I knew upon their return we were to revisit things so we could reverse temporary custody. So, she knew enough to know that this was a huge deal for me.

She said, "Well, what are you still doing here? Go!"

Everything in me was anxious. It was close to lunchtime and I took off the rest of the day and drove the two-hour distance to where they were. While driving, I prayed, I cried, I laughed at the thought of how long it had been but how soon it came to them coming back. I was hyped up and on overload.

Knocking on the door immediately brought back dark feelings. I hadn't darkened this doorstep in a very long time and didn't miss it one bit. My children were on the other side of the door, so I didn't care about anything else but seeing them and putting things back in place.

The door opened, and the kids were standing right there. As soon as they saw me, they ran out, and we embraced and cried. Immediately, their father interfered and made them go back into the house.

I looked at him as if he'd lost his mind. "Why did you make them go back in? I want to see my children!"

If looks could kill, I would have dropped dead on sight. "Your daughter, he said, waving his hand, as if writing her off, "you can have, but you will never have your son back again."

Just like that. Like she wasn't the firstborn, like no one witnessed all that happened with my health after giving birth or anything. Just like that, she was waved off. Just like that.

I said, "I'm sorry there is so much hatred toward me and I pray one day you will find forgiveness over what you felt I did so horrible."

I wanted to see my children and embrace them, look at them, study them to see the changes that had taken place. It was stolen from me. He ordered me off the property. I walked off, stood on the sidewalk, and I called the police.

Upon their arrival, I told them that my children just returned from overseas and our daughter called me to let me know and that I just drove two hours to see them. I asked him to assist me in seeing my kids. He went to the porch and was told that I was wanted off the property. The police officer told me I had to leave because I was trespassing. Even though I wanted to see the kids, he couldn't make it happen and it would have to play out in court. I thought, *Court! What! What type of human being am I dealing with?*

Even writing this, I can't go into detail as far as how I felt. It's too painful to rehash, but I said to all that stood there that I was going to pray for them and from my ex, to parents and the forced addition in his life, they all laughed at me as if I was a joke. Ignorance at its best. I felt like an outsider who had children, was a nurturing mother but cast out as if I never existed. I walked away and suddenly pictured the vision of the people who mocked Jesus as he was going to his death. I kid you not that, that day was when I felt his pain even though it was understood way before that moment. I felt the mockery, and it was earth-shattering.

I got back into my car and just wept. What reason did he give our children why I left? I wondered if they heard everything. I wanted to know if our daughter heard her being shooed off as if she wasn't as valuable as our son. If so, how was she feeling? So many thoughts went through my head and so many feelings had built up inside of me that I wanted to cause damage with no remorse. Hate grew in my heart toward the hate that was toward me when I wasn't the cause of things. All my pain returned from that day at the courthouse before Japan, the disconnection in communication with them, everything.

Unable to drive the two hours back home, I went to my mother's. I cried and was sick to my stomach. Again, I couldn't talk to my kids as I called my daughter's number, but it kept going to voicemail. When I returned home and to my every day, I was drained and empty. After being away from me for two years, my children were two hours away from me now, yet it still felt like they were in Japan...unreachable.

No more money to borrow and no more time to conjure up something to take him to court. I felt defeated day in and day out. I was fatigued. "This just cannot be happening, Lord," I often found myself saying. Why didn't I see this before I'd made the choices to connect with such a person? I honestly didn't see it. I felt all sorts of things about what was really going on before my eyes.

Just as always, the order to revisit things went ignored, and things were handled as if the courts had no power or say, and we were just going to do what we wanted. My son was now in another state because of new military orders and they left my daughter behind as if she was a burden. I cried out to God on her behalf about things that she was doing because I knew she was rebelling. I knew she was screaming for attention. I cried out for Him to cover her while she was lost and trying to fit in. She was looking for love in her own way and it killed my soul to watch.

Everything that transpired, blaming everyone else but the watchmen. My daughter was talked about to others and the usual acts of sainthood went noticed. I've listened to the watchmen say things and watched manipulation toward others with words and try putting thoughts into the minds of children about their parents, etc. I always vowed that it wouldn't happen to my children, and here we are. The dysfunction was real, but covered up by false spirituality.

I tried to get my daughter to come to stay with me. She was trying so hard to be an adult and on her own, that when the opportunity arose, she took and ran. As her mother, she knew I had rules and boundaries. She was making up her own mind and feeling her way through life, and things had just changed. Her outlook changed. I realized that the more I tried to tell her the truths about things; I started looking just like the bad guy, too. So, I stopped and had to let go. I didn't know what exactly happened to her while overseas, but she wasn't the same.

Going back home and to work was not easy. This didn't turn out at all the way I'd envisioned it. How could I have thought it would, though, dealing with what I was up against?

Finding my way through the red tape wasn't easy, but I pressed toward it being doable and only workable because I refuse to let go of my relationship with Jesus. Without Him, I would still be a total mess and a patient at the nearest mental institution. My grip on Him was and is for real.

CHAPTER FIFTEEN

Holding on to Invisible Strength

The enemy tried to break me with devious plans to take from me what I cherished dearly. My heartbeats. Okay, now what? It didn't matter who I vented or cried to, explaining how I was feeling, telling every detail of what was going on, just couldn't come out. I didn't have that type of time to give it all to one person. The only one who knew all without my telling all was Jesus. I had to give it to Him. My mind, my heart, my being, my walk, my talk, my every day because losing it was an understatement. I was losing myself, and who would believe me if I'd sat down and told every single thing? At times, I couldn't believe it myself. I was a mother without her children; precious time lost and stolen, that I would never get back.

I listened to sermons, holding onto every word of the Word I'd receive from church; uplifting songs and finding a friend within myself to talk to outside of talking to the Lord. There truly isn't a friend like Jesus. I didn't have to reason with myself or my guilt. I didn't have to tell Him what happened yesterday or the day before. I didn't have to remind Him of this day or that one. He already knew it all. So, I held onto that. My daily walk, going to work with a smile on my face, laughing with people and family, going shopping and out to eat with friends as if I was fine and living life yet again, as though I had it all together was all portrayed with invisible strength. It was déjà vu all over again.

Somehow, my daughter was convinced into joining Job Corps in the same state of new duty orders given and it blew my mind. I didn't understand why she couldn't see what was going on from the outside, but I chose not to point it out to her. I refused to be the villain in this. I refused to give attention to the needed source, nor was I going to come between that situation. It was as if the goal was to keep her out of the way but to make sure she wouldn't come back to me, either. The need for this attention was obvious and whatever was said would be gold to my daughter, if put in a manipulative way, seeming as if it was coming from a true place of love. Job Corps was not someplace she deserved to be in her life. She was a straight-A student with a high grade point average. What was the real angle in this suggestion over her life? It made me so sick.

I couldn't do anything but continue walking in my strength. In all this, there were never any conversations between their father and me. It was crazy to go through so much with a person and never talk to them. This has been my life upon leaving for most of my post-marriage. I strictly had to trust and rely on God to see me through this and to cover my children. Praying a lot was all I did consistently, holding on to Him for dear life for my mental place of stability and dealing with the disconnection between my children and me, and it was hard. Real hard.

Trying to figure out my life and what my next steps should be, I was working and received a call from my attorney, telling me another subpoena in the state I'd moved from was filed.

It was for back child support. Wow. Writing this at this moment, I can't do anything but laugh. Lord, I think there were many sleepless nights, wondering what else could he do toward me that would keep the flames going. When was the focus going to be placed on the reason I left in the first place? The freedom needed, the new people needed and the out that was needed that I gave. Why was he so hell-bent on focusing on getting to me in any way possible?

I'd adopted Subpoena as a part of my name and subpoena after subpoena filed with the courts turned into a wonder how the beginning, middle, and the end of it was going to be. I'd been back home at this point for two years and had become stronger in my relationship with Jesus. My faith was stronger, and I believed that no matter what came my way, I was unstoppable. There was a purpose in this madness, even though I couldn't see it. Even though I feared never having my children in my life again, I believed in the power of God. They were getting older. The time I gave up was the time I needed, especially for my daughter, to continue molding and influencing. Well, I don't know if this was my being righteous-minded or what, but based on all that I'd witnessed, I surely didn't want them to follow the type of hearts like those they were exposed to. I don't know; it was just a crazy situation all around and here we go again.

Upon hearing this, I had to figure out how I was going to afford to go backward. I had to set up an over-the-phone session so I could state my whereabouts and my financial situation. During this phone session, I was told that I needed to be physically present or the decision would be made without me and that I would have to pay whatever was calculated, whether I agreed with it or not. I asked if I was going to see my son as I hadn't seen him and was told that it was a child support hearing and the adults should be able to work this out amongst themselves. Well, that was out of the window, so I knew I wouldn't get to see him.

Between the date of the court hearing and my working out how I was going to make this trip affordable without putting anyone else in the middle of my chaos, I'd spoken with my daughter. She told me that once she left to go to Job Corps, which was an hour from where duty orders were given, a little after she arrived, he'd placed orders for retirement near the place where my children planted their roots in Tennessee. Where we were moving forward and living our lives before the chaos hit. This is where my son wanted to come back to, to be close to what he considered his home, where he'd gone to elementary and middle school and met his best friend. It was home to them.

So, now she would be in this area alone with no family around. I was crushed that she still couldn't see what was going on. I didn't point it out, but in my heart, I was just devastated over it.

I vented to my Father when I couldn't hold it in anymore, instead of venting to others. He'd been there from the start and saw all truths in the whole situation, and getting me through my tears.

Retiring forty-five minutes from where I used to reside with our children before all of this began to happen. Our children loved where we were. My son, through conversations with his sister, wanted to come back to me. He wanted to be back home. So, the move was made close enough to give access to what was missed to deviate what was wanted. It was also known that even though I wasn't on the same financial level, I wouldn't give up trying to get back what was taken from me. My children. Discernment is beautiful when you are connected. I saw right through it all.

I understood this wasn't anyone else's fight but mine, and I needed my son in my life. I accomplished my purpose of my moving back home, and I didn't need anyone's understanding or approval for what I was going through and needed to do whether it made sense to them or not. It was me and God. That's it.

My lease was soon up and I moved back down south. I'd be back in time for court and to build back a relationship with my son. My daughter was still in Job Corps and would work on that situation once I'd gotten settled if there was anything that I could do to change it. The court date was coming up soon, and I needed to decide what I was going to do besides court, once I returned.

Speaking with a girlfriend of mine from the company where I worked before moving back up north about my situation, she invited me to stay with her until I could find a place. This was a tremendous blessing and less I had to worry about. I packed up my house, put my things in storage at my mother's and drove back down south.

The child support agency filed an order as if there were never any conversation about reversing things upon my children's return. As if to say that now, not only was I not getting my son back, but I will have to pay child support from here on out. The sad thing was that I simply had no money to fight things and no attorney to bring this back to court to turn things around. I was at a loss and I literally felt my back up against the wall with nowhere to turn. But God.

Money isn't everything, but it is something when you need it to take care of circumstances such as this. I had to rely on God to handle things. My relationship was solid with Him and I was confident, even with my nerves running everywhere, that He was going to come through for me somehow. I wasn't sure how, but I just believed He would because I became His when I said, "Yes." to Him.

Arriving at my girlfriend's house and getting settled in, we had time to catch up, and she went above and beyond to show her hospitality to me. She is a beautiful person with a heart as big as this world and I will forever be grateful to her for opening her home to me. She gave me the room to do what I needed to do to get my feet planted again without thinking twice about it. At every turn, I saw God working even in my tears I shed in the middle of so many involuntary fights. I was still human, and I still wanted to dish out what I was receiving, but I didn't. I literally let Him move the mountains for me no matter what it looked like.

Court was coming up in a couple of months, and I was there to appear. I had only a small window to figure out what to do, where to report to for such a case, and how to fill out the required paperwork I was told I needed to fill out and had no attorney. I needed to find out what my chances were at even being heard regarding the true reasoning behind this. I needed to say something about the reverse custody, behaviors, etc. In the past, my voice wasn't exactly what the judges wanted to hear with no representation, so the closer the date came, the more nauseous and prayerful I became. I just wanted it to go away.

I'd gained my peace back, my stability mentally, and started healing and now it seemed I was right back in the trauma of shenanigans. Even so, I had to step up and face this because it wasn't going away. My girlfriend asked if I wanted her to take off work to go with me down to the courthouse. I thanked her for the offer but told her that this was my fight. I had God with me and He was going to walk with me through this, so I wasn't as tormented as before. I wasn't alone.

As I recap on things, I still can't believe it was me who was dealing with such monstrosity. I wouldn't dare wish it was someone else, but to know that it was my truth, my secret wounds, was so crazy. Never knowing the capabilities of a person who you shockingly found out that you were all wrong about never got old. There was never a dull moment, unfortunately. I felt sorry for those who couldn't simply move on with their lives. I also felt tired because it was at my expense.

I'm not sure if you, who are reading this, can relate to anything I've been through or are living something like it right now. If you are, I empathize with you, but I pray for strength over your life even while it may be invisible to eyes that lay on you every day…stay planted. If you aren't quite planted, it's never too late to become planted and try God at His Word. He is not a man who lies. Remember when we used to convince somebody that we were telling them the truth about a certain situation and we would say, "Man, I put that on everything I love?" This is how God feels about His Word over us. He wants to convince us that we can put all He promised on Him because He's telling us the truth about all He can and will do in our lives. I'm a living witness to the power and the strength I received in my life during such dark times. I'm holding onto the same invisible strength to this very day. It's never over until God says so.

Immediately, I started looking for work. I needed to get things in order with moving back and to find my own place along with the fact that before going to court, I would need income to prove I was indeed working. I'd found an odd job to do here and there and then tried going back to the company I'd left. I guess this wasn't my first thought because I'd left a basket case and felt like all the drama I had going on and, with it being well known, would cause some hesitance in rehiring me. However, I was a great employee who did the work and outside of my situation; I held my head up and had a good reputation, was always on time, and did what I had to do while there. Giving them a two-week notice before leaving made a difference as well, so I took the chance of calling human resources. I needed income before going before a judge, especially with no attorney. I could at least speak and say that I had employment.

Praying before reaching out to my old employer and reaching a familiar voice on the other end of the phone, instantly the man remembered me. He said, "Hey, Kim!" I'd explained what I needed, and he told me he would check into it for me and to call him back in a couple of days. I did this and was told that upon him informing Human Resources of my return and the open positions needed, several managers asked for me. I felt more than grateful. I felt more than blessed. We set up an appointment to meet for an interview. I went through the appropriate steps and they rehired me. Praise God! He continued to work with every step I made.

Now that I'd obtained employment and had a few weeks before starting, my confidence was better and I could find a place of my own. I needed to do as much as I could before work. I didn't want to start work and allow my old activities to become familiar and repeated activities dealing with court.

Before my day in court, I went to the courthouse with nothing in my hand but my subpoena for child support court. As I drove into a parking space, I sat there and talked with Jesus. "Lord, I'm going in with You and You know I have no clue as to what to do so I'm trusting that You have a plan because I don't. So here we go." I know there are cases where the mother is the one who is being taken to court for this, but honestly, somehow, I felt insulted and embarrassed. The type of mother that I had always been with my children and this whole thing just kept throwing me off into a spinning wheel. I knew I was closer to Jesus and had surrendered parts of me I hadn't met before because of doing things my way for so long. But here I was in the courthouse feeling again like this bullied victim that couldn't prove the things that were happening to me and the bully kept getting away with everything.

As I walked into the building through the double doors, a slender lady who looked as if she could be of Jewish descent held the door open for me. She was dressed in an expensive-looking suit, walking in the same direction as I was, with her briefcase in one hand and a cup of coffee in the other. I said, "Thank you," as I kept walking toward the metal detectors. I went through as required, placing my things on the belt, walked through, and proceeded to the corridor to look up in the square glass case on the wall for the location I needed to get to. Finding what I assumed to be the correct office to get the help I needed, I rode the elevator to that floor and walked into that office, and stepped up to the counter. As I started to speak, I realized that all the anxiety I was holding in had become too much and instead of speaking, I broke into tears. I couldn't stop and couldn't speak.

I didn't even see it coming, nor did I know where to begin. I always had to figure out a plan to be represented and either the money came from my mother or others helped by chipping in. I just couldn't do that anymore. I didn't want to continue receiving funds from others because of another person. I broke. I didn't plan on breaking, but I did. Everything I'd experienced came out right there at that counter and I couldn't breathe.

Each employee behind the desk looked up at me, baffled along with sympathetic expressions, and asked if I were okay and how they could help me. Before I could say anything, a petite, beautiful Black elderly woman came from behind the counter and took my hand, leading me out into the hallway. She looked me in the face and said, "It's going to be all right." She handed me some Kleenex and guided me to a spot to cool down and stood with me. Once I could speak, I told her what I needed, that I had no representation and I didn't know where to begin.

She asked me some questions regarding my situation and the history of things. There was no way I could explain to her all that I'd gone through. We got acquainted, and I spoke with her often. Still, with no representation, she told me I could use a court-appointed lawyer from another clerk, but my chances would be better if I got a lawyer that wasn't appointed.

As we were talking, the same lady that held the door for me to enter the building approached us. It was obvious that she and the lady who was consoling me were long-time acquaintances. They greeted each other and joked about their evening with each other and their spouses, so they were close friends outside of work.

Turning back toward me, she assured me that God will work things out and that I needed to trust Him. She told me to read Proverbs 31 (The Virtuous Woman) and to meditate on it, gave me the paperwork I needed to fill out and bring back, gave me a huge mother bear hug and I teared up again.

Once I reached the double doors to leave out of the building, the same lady who held the doors for me stopped me. She said, "Hi, do you mind if I talked to you for a second?" I said, "No, not at all." As we walked outside toward my car, she asked me what I was looking for. I gave her a brief rundown of my court life and history up to that point and that I simply couldn't afford to obtain representation anymore and that I'd just started back working at my old employer.

She said she was so sorry to hear about my situation. She said that she couldn't stand bullies as she saw it all the time in court with the people she would have to defend. After this, she took out her card and told me to call her and that even though she charged an amount that she knew I couldn't afford she would still help me and that we could work something out later with cost and it wouldn't be even close to what she usually charged. I held it together as I took her card and thanked her from the bottom of my heart.

When I got in my car, I broke down, thanking God for hearing me and expediently placing the right people in my life on this path. From that moment on, I saw hope through this situation. Unsure of how I was going to get things back on track, I held on. My daughter was now away from me and our son wasn't back home with me even though they were back in the states.

I felt as though I was doing the right thing by our children, by allowing them the opportunity to experience things and to give them a chance to see how it was being with the other parent. The decision was already tough enough knowing that I would not see them after so long and after the charades that happened when it was only going to be our son and plans conjured up with my daughter; it was all so ludicrous. This was all too much to take in on every level. I was sick to my stomach at the thought of it all. My tears were tired of my tears, I cried so much. It was plain awful.

Now that I knew I had representation in this child support hearing, my mind was at ease outside of waiting to hear how much this was going to cost. I prayed, kept talking to God about things, and taking one day at a time. God showed me He had me and no matter what and how it felt, I would be okay. The enemy feeds on how things look and sound to others. God feeds on truths. I stopped dwelling on how I looked to anyone because only a handful of people knew the truth of the ill intentions.

My attorney requested from the courts to reschedule the hearing so she could come up to speed with the case and our past court appearances.

Moving back down south, I had money saved, plus what I drew from my job I'd left, so I had a cushion to play with. Thanks to my friend, letting me stay with her was more than a blessing while I returned to my old employer. With this, I could use the money I had to start paying this attorney. Once she looked over the history of my being taken to court and the reasons behind it, she said, "What a loser." She then said that her cost was minimal for me because this was blatant bullying. Her cost was more than reasonable and I could take care of it. Praise God for *favor!*

We went to court on the rescheduled date and by this time I'd started work, so I had to take a day off to go. It all felt so surreal. You know how you get kind of hot under the collar and start feeling the pressure with sweating? This was me on that day and I had to go alone with no support team.

During the hearing, folks did all they could to get my attention: throat clearing, talking, and laughing out loud like they were at a comedy show. I refused to entertain them. I looked all around the courtroom while sitting and waiting to be called to the stand, focusing on every wood-carved setting in the ceiling of the courtroom. The designs in the carpet, the words behind the judge's chair that said, "In God We Trust," and thinking to myself, *Yes, I am trusting in You to get me through this.* I had to turn in all bank statements, receipts of my spending, and check stubs from my job. Both attorneys and the judge already examined all documents.

Before starting, they would only allow those who needed to be in to come in. Upon waiting to start, the judge kept looking at me and then at the other party. He witnessed what had been going on with the homemade party to get my attention. I never gave in. The judge shut whatever folder he had in front of him and said, "I'd like to see both attorneys in my chambers immediately, please." I saw it coming because the show in the courtroom was comical.

He wanted to avoid anything having to be said because he saw the vulgarity displayed toward me and I just sat there looking straight ahead. He attempted to settle the case without a hearing to see if both attorneys could simply come up with a planned amount for support based on the info given. however, the opposing attorney wanted a hearing, but my attorney was open to settling. He was trying to avoid the slander that obviously awaited.

So, the judge returned along with our attorneys and stated that the attempt at settling went unsuccessful and that we would have to proceed with the hearing.

Exactly what the judge had witnessed and was trying to avoid was confirmed by the first person on the stand. I was deemed unstable and unfit to continue taking care of our children upon the attorneys off the wall questions as to why child support was being sought. The judge said, "This is not a character case and I will not permit any defamation of character. What is it that you are seeking for support? This is what this hearing is about." I focused on the judge or an object above his head, thinking to myself, *Really? Unstable?* Why, because of intimidation of someone you didn't know and used to your advantage over what was already over?

The asking amount was $480 a month, plus costs for court. The opposing attorney asked if arrears could be awarded and the judge gave her client the choice to turn it down or accept. It was accepted and requested it not only be for our son but for the time my daughter was overseas too since she was of age now and it couldn't be collected monthly for her. His attorney asked if this could be calculated in things as well. My attorney stated that based on my income, it was not acceptable and that I should not have to pay court costs because I wasn't the one initiating the hearing.

It was my turn now to get on the stand. While on the stand, I focused on the rooftop outside the window, watching bird after bird land and fly away because no one deserved the satisfaction of even connecting stares. I didn't allow any hideous smirks or anything. The opposing attorney tried to piggyback on attempting to attack my character and the judge, again, altered the questioning and ordered things to gear only toward the reason of the hearing.

So, the adversary went after my spending by assessing my bank statement. She said, "So, I see that you like eating out a lot and there are multiple amounts on here that say, 'Tithes.' You're not big on saving, are you?"

I said to her, "You don't know me. You are going by what is being said to you and there's not a lot of facts to it but I don't have to defend myself to you."

She then said, "You allowed your children to go overseas and signed permission because you would rather spend the time with the friend you have than be with your children."

I simply laughed at this because they were so out in left field, trying so hard to prove something. I said, "Ma'am, move on because I'm not going to entertain the ignorance that you are attempting. Why this is still even something that's on the forefront should answer all of this court's questions. That's not even a question. It's a slick attempt to make a statement but I can answer no to it anyway."

I didn't even take the time out to explain that we weren't even together anymore because it simply wasn't their business. My relationship back then was the sole reason we were here today. If I had become a hermit, I would have never become best friends with the court system. NEXT!

My attorney objected to each statement made, and the judge got irritated and stated that if we couldn't stick to the true meaning of the hearing then he would end it and make the decision himself. He stated to me that by looking at my statement he concurred that I should bring to a minimum my tithing and said that it wasn't considered appropriate when I could cut it down for cost purposes.

I stated, "Tithing is something that I'm going to do with the money that I go to work for that I was blessed to have, so that wasn't going to be altered." I also stated that I was never unstable nor an unfit person and that I am a great mother and have always been just that. I stated that I couldn't support what I couldn't reach. I bought up the fact of being cut out of our children's lives through communication and against the court's orders.

The judge had heard enough and stated that he had other cases that needed his attention and that we needed to come to an agreement on what we were there for. I came down from the stand and an amount was agreed upon monthly along with arrears included, but no court costs were going to be collected from me. I said to my attorney, "Can I go now?" She said yes, and that it was all over and to make sure I took care of things with my employer so that they could take the amount out automatically. I agreed and walked out and walked away.

Even though I walked out with a smile on my face, I was full. When I got outside, I wept. I wept for so many reasons. I was sweaty and hot-headed over the sickness of it all that I still had to endure with such unhappy people. I got myself together after getting in my car and sitting there for a minute. I thought of how happy it was being free to live and not have to pretend to be happy. I was happy that our son would soon be an adult and there would be nothing else left to conjure up against me. My tears dried up, and I had to move on. I switched gears in giving thanks because even in my somberness, God has been right there.

Thank you, Lord, for walking with me. Thank you for allowing me to have representation and being able to share the most pertinent information with my attorney in such a short period of time. Thank you for giving me the strength to face my adversary with boldness and not break down in front of them like in past times. Thank you for giving me the maturity and legs to walk out and pass up opportunities that I would have taken before to make snide remarks. Thanks for loving me and keeping me through it all. Thanks for my sanity in an insane situation. Thanks.

CHAPTER SIXTEEN

Old Bruises, New Armor

I forgave. I forgave more than once through all I'd dealt with in and outside of my marriage. I have relived so many things in my life as far as relationships that holding on to all the flashbacks became detrimental. So, with the help of God pruning me, I started learning from it. When I truly built my relationship with Christ, forgiving became second nature. He showed me what being unforgiving did to my health, my mind, my relationship with Him, as well as those close to me. It was tiring not forgiving because it kept me in victim mode.

It wasn't worth fighting the child support. My daughter was experiencing life as a young adult and my son would soon be out of high school. I wanted him to come back to me still, but hadn't spoken to him to see how he was feeling or what was going on with him. He was living forty-five minutes from me and he didn't know it. How they were doing was my only concern. When I went to see them upon returning to the states, my only concern was knowing the state of their minds. If charging arrears on me was needed to feel better, I felt better, too, at that point. All I knew was that it was over as far as facing judges, my adversary, and hatred. I wasn't rich financially, but I was rich spiritually and it was going to be covered.

Our son was sixteen. He was at the age where he could speak for himself and was even working, so he could say what he wanted to do without the court's approval. My mission was to connect with him somehow. So, I relied on Jesus to do what He does. Work it out and He did in the parking lot of Walmart.

Three years had passed with my not being in either of my children's lives. So much time away and the influence deposited into them with my being a missing link in the chain was unthinkable.

I was still staying with my friend. After going back to my old job and working a while, I started looking for a place to stay. The place where I was before moving back home had vacancies. However, I was nervous to try them since I'd broken my lease. The same apartments I'd moved into when I moved out from living with the friend I was with at that time. We'd lived there together in another section of the complex after moving out of the house. Once I looked at a few places, I prayed about it and asked God to walk with me in inquiring about going back. I called and told the person who answered the phone who I was and immediately she remembered me and my issues before leaving. Praise God for the empathy she showed toward things then and said, "Sure, Kimberly, you paid your rent on time and was never a problem. I knew why you left and we'd love to have you back as a renter." God is good! First my old job welcomed me back with open arms and now this.

I have much gratitude toward my girlfriend, who allowed me to stay with her for as long as I needed. I'm blessed beyond measure with people chosen to be on my journey with me as He orchestrated my walk. So blessed.

After moving into my apartment and working, I returned to the church I attended before I left. Getting settled in felt awesome. I was decorating and happy to be back, along with looking forward to rebuilding where I could with my children. I remember being in the bedroom one day watching television and thinking about the months that had gone by without still being able to see my son, who was so close but so far. I was happy my daughter had transitioned from Job Corps to AMERICORP. I could tell a vast difference in her tone and felt her happiness through the phone. It was like taking a deep breath and exhaling through one part and still hoping and praying through another. However, on this day, the anxiety of not seeing my son got the better part of me.

Not knowing how returning to be close to my son and possibly see my daughter again was going to manifest stayed at the forefront of my thoughts. We considered this our stomping ground as this was where most of the childhood memories started with them—schoolmate relationships and overall things that matter to a child in being stable and set in finding their growing individualities. It was home for us. I kept believing and trusting that being here was better than not being here. Being isolated back home was for my good, and I knew it. I built a relationship with myself as well as with God and got to know me for the first time in over fifteen-plus years. It was for my good. I had to trust the process.

Sometimes, I was in a situation that was too far gone to recover. I wondered whether starting with my children right where we were was a figment of my imagination. I kept thinking back on the day they left and how deep of a cut that was and how I could not bear to feel that type of pain again. For a long time, I continued to see my son's face when it was ordered that he was to go overseas. Those eyes looked at me with so much love and hope of understanding that he wanted to see what it was like to be with his dad and to experience another part of the world. He looked at me as if he were pleading with me not to be hurt while he was hurting, too. I thought about how deep the cut was for them to have even gone through such choices. Those beautiful little faces I was missing so desperately and although they weren't so little anymore, they were still my babies and will always be.

A part of me was numb to a lot of things but also saw that maybe they needed to see the other side of things since my marriage had ended. I took it personally at first but also didn't want to take away their chances to see what they asked for and as a mother, being hands-on with them all their lives, the decision was more than difficult. It was devastatingly hard. I hadn't expected to miss a beat in their lives, just as the judge had ordered. It was like I was scratched out of their lives and wasn't the one who'd given birth to them. It felt like I no longer mattered.

The thoughts about the role I played in what possibly caused them to want to switch to living with the other parent and all that had transpired held my attention. While wanting to move on with my life, I made the mistake of not including them in adding to our family, but assuming they would be okay with it came to mind often. The relationship didn't end up the way I pictured or went as planned, but I felt I had the right to live my life, whether there were ups or downs in it. It wasn't their fault or anyone else's. It was a plan that wasn't well thought out and they became children in the middle of a war they never asked for.

I was tired of replaying so much of the past in my head. I was sick of feeling like I did something wrong to cause this whole charade. What else was I supposed to learn about this? I certainly learned my lesson and I certainly earned the title, "Healed." So, how was I ending up alone and isolated yet again?

Out of nowhere, the tears started rolling down my face and I cried out to Jesus, telling Him that my heart was hurting. I needed to see my son. I wanted to see my daughter, who was away living her own life and although I was so proud of her, I stood in need. I don't remember how long this conversation with Him lasted, but I poured out all my hurt in not having my children in my life and the time frame it had been. I curled up tighter where I was sitting and sat there for a while in my feelings and His presence. Even though He already knew what was in my heart, I needed to confess it out loud because holding it in made my chest feel like it was going to explode. Jesus wants to hear from us out loud. I had to confess with my mouth and speak outwardly even though I knew He knew my steps before I ever made them. So, I talked to Him outwardly amid my tears and snot.

That same day, I went to the store and pulled into a parking space at Walmart. I saw my son in my peripheral vision. He and his longtime friend, from grade school, were parking two spaces from me at the same time! Jesus answered me just like that! I jumped out so fast when I saw him; I had to jump back in to put my car into park. His eyes welled up and so did mine. A totally unforgettable moment. He was so tall and handsome. Seeing him again and all the thoughts and feelings that were like mine were visible on his face and it felt like I was dreaming. Like, Lord, we just talked about this. So am I here in the flesh right now? I needed this and the Lord knew it.

He said he saw me first, and that's why he was walking toward me. We walked into the store after talking and hugging for a bit and I spoke to his friend who remembered me and we briefly caught up. They were just killing time before going to play basketball at his friend's church and were trying to give their other friends time to meet them. Look at God! Just awesome! We took pictures together right there in the store and made plans for him to visit me. *Hallelujah!* I didn't want to let him go, and he didn't want the moment to end either, but it was time for them to meet up with their friends. We hugged each other so tightly and said our see-you-laters because it wasn't goodbye.

I slept like a baby that night and my heart was full and anticipated our meet again. I thanked Him for loving me so much and instantaneously blessing me. Blessing me at being able to touch my son and hold him again, even if it was only for a while. It felt like forever.

My praise was in overflow. God is so good, and He really comes right on time, even when it may not be when we want Him to. He knows how the timing should go. It was one of the best days I'd seen outside of knowing that my daughter was now where she really wanted to be and moving on with her life in a great way. This gave my moving back more inspiration and definition to where I didn't have to keep questioning what I was doing. I trusted and walked by faith that my children and I would one day reunite. I had to trust that the reason for the space wasn't solely based on taking from me, but on growth from my Father toward me.

Unfortunately, my son and I had to agree that he wouldn't mention that he saw me. He wanted nothing to get in the way of our meeting and catching up. My son could hang out with his friends as they were all where I lived, so they would pick him up. Upon knowing that he would come to see me was something we felt would have been interrupted. So, I had to wait until the next time his friends picked him up and brought him my way again. He said that he did not know I was back, nor did he know anything about court. He thought I was still living back in Indiana. I told him why I moved back and that it was solely because of him and his sister.

Upon sight, I wanted my son back. I was elated but understood that processes are a way of life and I saw Him working while I was walking on this journey. That was a good day, and I wished it could have lasted longer, but I got it. Patience is a virtue. I was holding onto Jesus' leg for dear life while going through my new chapters on unforeseen things.

Things were sustainable after seeing my son and being able to at least speak with my daughter over the phone from time to time. From the day I saw him, we spoke daily. My moving back to be closer became clearer. I didn't care about anything else outside of being able to reach out and physically see and touch my kids.

Unbeknownst to me, long roads were ahead in trying to catch up on where we'd left off when they went overseas. My son told me he wished he knew I was there because all the time I'd been there, he was coming each weekend to spend with his friends. He'd said that he could have been spending that time at my house, too.

Time went by and he was coming by the house. We'd watch a movie, go out to eat, or just hung out, but was doing it secretly. It did not thrill me because I'm his mother. I prayed God would work it out, and I trusted him. Suddenly, his visits to see his friends faded, and I'd started relying on them just to see him. I'd ask him when the next time he'd be coming that way. He had said that he was tired of hiding the fact that he saw me and he wanted to come and stay with me for the weekend, so he made it aware that he saw me at the store. From that point on, his visits stopped and his friends had to come to him to visit if they wanted to hang out.

Well, it came to pass that my son had announced that he wanted to live with me once he found out I was back and after he saw me at the store. He told me that once he'd mentioned this, it was the end of him coming my way.

Not seeing him lasted for quite a while and I had chosen not to fight for visitation or anything. I learned through all this ordeal that Satan was happily orchestrating these ill-gotten actions and it wasn't the actual person behind it all; it was the enemy that was being allowed in the person to continue to hold on to things. I just let God work. I'd been through enough and had cried enough to build a whole personal Niagara Falls in my backyard. It was time out for this. Momentarily, I regretted not going through with setting in place visitation rights, but my son was no baby and I chose not to do it. When I spoke to my son, I asked him what he thought about my modifying this with the courts. He said, "Mom, it's okay, you don't have to go through that. I'm going to just let it be known that I want to move." We did some research on him transferring schools and during this process, other strategies were being planned out as well.

The way things had played out, I had to keep trusting God to work them out. My son and I were researching the transference in schools as my son's birthday was coming up and we'd have to get him settled if he were going to move.

While doing this, he received the offer to get a car for his birthday. We both knew the reason for this offer, but my son told me he'd said, "Well, hypothetically if it's a birthday gift, I can still take it with me to Mom's house, right?" He told me that even though the answer was yes, he was asked why. My son stated he was just wanting to make sure. Well, he never received the car for his birthday. During the process of our researching as it was now a week before school was to start, we found out that if he were to transfer, he'd have to redo classes he'd already taken.

He was a year ahead in school already and this was going to be his senior year when he would outside of this be a junior. My children were always great students and achievers in school with perfect attendance until they were taken out for court reasons. We both had decided that it was in his best interest to stay where he was and continue through his last year because the oncoming senior classes he was to have would only be two. If he came to stay with me, he'd have more classes to repeat, along with regular senior classes. It was two different school districts and rules.

I was on cloud nine as we could catch up and hang out. School was starting, and I was kind of sad that he couldn't move with me. I was so hopeful, but to think about all my children had endured, through it all, they maintained their grades in school even when things were tough for them and they were dealing with things on their level and in their way. We were all on emotional roller coaster rides back then and they stayed grounded through school. Mentally, I know it wasn't easy for them, so to have made it through without acting out, becoming disrespectful, and getting into trouble was a profound blessing.

Thanking the Lord that He heard me cry out to Him and instantly worked in my favor, I watched the floodgates of extended favor given to having my children back in my life. That made my heart glad that the connections flowed again. I was thankful to have them back in my life. I was thankful that GOD kept pursuing me to where I still have my life and hadn't taken it through my suicidal thoughts prematurely.

Learning what his favorite color was now, the things he liked to do, how he thought about certain things felt kind of funny because I used to know. Things change as we grow, so I was taking it all in, watching a new outlook on life through his eyes, and it was everything to me. Sometimes it would appear he was nonchalant about things, loving and so respectful as I remembered, and at times in his eyes, there seemed to be no light. Overall, I understood, but stayed in prayer and as connected with him as possible. He grew up into such a wonderful young man with the same patience he's always had with situations.

During a conversation with my daughter, she told me that her brother had adopted an "I don't really care attitude." I asked her what she meant, and she said that ever since things were so crazy, it was what he would tell her. Without telling her, it hurt to hear more than she will ever know. He'd always been a happy kid. He was always so open and spoke freely to me. I knew he wasn't angry with me, but life happened and I went at his pace at moving through it.

He had friends he went to school with back in his life, and that made him happy. I was happy to see him walking around the house when he'd stay with me over the weekends and paying attention to details of where he was mentally.

During catching up, there was still the reality of the need to address issues in order to move forward. I wasn't sure how it would go, so I waited for him to bring things up, as he eventually did here and there. We talked about my friend moving in and he told me how he and his sister felt about it. They never wanted my friend to move in with us but dealt with it because they thought it made me happy. They liked him as long as he was in his own place and not ours. My son was the little man of the house and he felt that was gone once the move in took place. He also said that even though there would be questions about stuff that went on in our home when they visited their father and him changing all they said around, he didn't care about that more than he cared about feeling like everything just changed unfairly.

He also asked me if I signed my parental rights over when they left because he said that was what they were told. I told him it was untrue and I took out all the paperwork from the courts to show that I signed only because of what he wanted and the permission I had to give by signing for passports. When I showed him, he smiled and said he never believed it because he knew I would do nothing like that, but he just had to ask. I was glad he asked, so the question wouldn't hang over his head unanswered. I told him I would never do such a thing and apologized for them having gone through all that chaos. I told him that had I known back then how they felt about moving someone in, I would have reversed it immediately with no questions asked.

He wanted to know about the things he'd heard about pictures being sent to me regarding the invitation to a wedding and a photo of a ring sent to my phone because he was told that it wasn't true. I pulled the invitation out and the picture to prove that it was indeed all true. When he looked at it, he simply handed it back and that was it. I didn't add or take away anything that needed validation between him and me. We simply moved forward and never talked about it again.

My children had grown and were going about their lives, and how it was handed to them. Despite the odds, they beat them. It took a long, long time for me to forgive myself for my part in things and to understand that I couldn't go back and change a thing. All I could do was move forward and allow God to work while I lived through it and love on my babies. My mother told me that no matter how hard I tried to go back in time, time had moved forward and they were older, with a different mindset and different influences that were planted over that time frame. So, I embraced the days we were in and let go.

Mental warfare is very real. I know this all too well as I was recovering from it. Now I was starting my journey again mothering. Even though it was mothering from a distance, I was happy. I kept those who loved me around me, who supported me with me, and God who always kept me in my darkest and lowest hours. It wasn't always peaches and cream, but I was still here in one piece and my children were, too. There was obvious healing that was needed and I was grateful for the opportunity to reach it no matter how long it took.

God showed me another side when I retreated backward in my thoughts. He showed me what I could be dealing with when the local news would announce children dying from random gunshots, being trafficked, having to live homeless, and mothers in despair over the loss of their children. Yes, He occasionally had to remind me of the grace and mercy. Chhhiiillleee, (as my girl Sarah Jakes-Roberts would say), I got whippings a lot from my Father and I felt them. Still do. It didn't mean that I couldn't hurt or be angry over things. It meant that if I asked Him to move on my behalf and give me strength that I couldn't go back on my word in saying that I trusted and believed He could keep me while on this journey. He told me I didn't have time to keep this victim mentality over situations. He had this in the palm of His hands. He had *power* and I would just need to have faith that all things would work together for my good. I needed to own that truth. The enemy (Satan) will make it appear as though it's a win because of what things look like; he knows this is the world's system. It's about perception over truth. So, this was my strength instead of my taking it as a weakness.

This book is a small window of all I've gone through. I missed my children and thankful that He kept them through my faults, my experiences, my depression, my missteps, my regrets, my disappointments, my pain, and my prayers and covered them in my absence. I can't go back to change a thing, and why would I? I couldn't learn without the lesson.

Spending this time with my son was an unexplainable feeling. Once it was clear he would be coming to see me, the mind games started. During the school year, my son would want to come to see me or his friends for the weekend and he'd be dropped off initially and I had to take him back. It was nice that it was seemingly thought out to where we were working together on his behalf, still without communicating. I felt it was fair to drive the forty-five minutes to take him back, so it was thought to be a great gesture. This changed suddenly, with him telling me the only way he could visit me was if drove forty-five minutes to pick him up and took him back. Wanting to see him as much as I could, it worked for a little while but got old quickly as each time going and coming it was like he was five and people had to stand in the door watching and staring to make sure he got in the car okay.

I stopped doing it because it became creepy too much and the civility of working together as parents wasn't the intent after all. Still. So, my son had to understand that I was no taxicab and that although I loved seeing him every chance I got, there had to be some cooperation in transportation. Not to mention that all the while he was with me, there was this need to face time with him, asking if he was okay, as if he was with a stranger and not his mother. Finally, I asked my son if this was a normal thing when he spent time with his friends and he said, "No." I knew the answer already but wanted to confirm it. While face-timing, the talks were loud in case I was in the vicinity. I heard, "If you go over your friends, that's where you better be and stay." It was entertaining because all I cared about was that I could be with my son. Before my son knew I was here, he said he would simply be dropped off at his friend's house to stay the weekend and the requirement to meet any of their parents was never warranted.

I learned firsthand about him wanting to go hang out at his friend's house and I told him I hadn't changed with wanting to know who he was going to be with and where they lived, how they were living, etc. While he was on my watch, we had to do things this way and when I took him, his old-time friend's mother was in the yard and I introduced myself. The first thing she said was, "I'm so happy to finally meet one of his parents." I asked her why and she said, "Well, your son is always over here and has stayed for days and I always wondered what parent would allow their kid to just stay somewhere without wanting to meet the parents or get to know us." She said, "He's such a gentleman and a good kid, so I just wondered who would just allow him to stay anywhere without wanting to know anything." I apologized and briefly explained my absenteeism and assured her this was not how I operated when it came to my children. We talked for a while about when the kids were smaller and the school they'd met at and how we never got to meet back then in passing during pick-up and drop-off times for school.

Once the realization hit that his moving with me would not happen, months later he received a car passed down from within the family. We were happy; he still got the car and could come to see me or his friend's and had transportation for work, so God continued to work everything out.

Talking with my daughter regularly now, her sending me pictures of her adventures in AmeriCorps and how happy she was, made it so much easier to deal with her not being around but having the connection often. Having my son back was more than I could have wanted. I saw God working. It may have not been how I'd planned it all out with them coming back to the states, but I honestly struggled to respect it and stayed obedient. I wanted things to just be right and to be cool. They were older now and moving on with plans for their own lives. Quickly realizing this as time spent over the phone with my daughter and spending this time with my son, I had no time for any extra and no time I wanted to waste on anything outside of positivity. It was the only way to go because He'd gotten me through a lot of awful times and brought my children back to me.

Going out to eat, shopping, cooking for him, and just hanging out watching movies was heaven with my son. Talking to my daughter about her relationships, her downfalls, hard times, being able to advise her, catching up on all she went through while away in Japan, was the other piece of heaven given to me. Nothing was more important than this. We were where God meant for us to be. We had our circle back, even though it returned with scars and growing pains; it came back airtight with understanding, forgiveness, and acceptance.

It would hurt many times when it was time for him to leave. I went through different times of regret and feeling like a mother who wasn't hands-on full time in his life. It was hard dealing with all the schematic things that had taken place, but I was reminded repeatedly of the blessing in all the enemy tried to hinder.

I swallowed many big pills along the way of having him back in my life and monkey wrenches thrown into the mix to deter things. Why? I didn't understand, but didn't allow it to change me or what was important.

Upon our building and every time our son needed some repairs on his car, needing something for school before it let out over the pandemic, or him wanting something, he would be told to ask me for half of the cost. Right before the Coronavirus was nationwide, I'd bought our son a suit for his prom that he never wore and we just agreed that he at least owned a nice new black suit. It wasn't cheap but was necessary for the occasion that he never got to attend.

It wasn't about my not wanting to do these things. As his mother, I was going to make sure he had what he needed. However, when it came to his car needing work, looking and researching different avenues on it being executed seemed to be hard for others to do for him. Yes, the thought had crossed my mind about wanting to take them from me but the work it took to put in on taking on this full time pursuit seemed to be too much to go the extra mile as a parent when needed. This came from many observations when my son needed help, which made me wonder about what took place with them in my absence.

Immediately, I clarified he would and should not be the relayer of messages. I was open to communicating, so long as it wasn't like the past—never hearing me and always in attack mode. I remained open and extended the offer of communication, but it never happened. So, I simply parented on my end and was fine with it.

He didn't even know I was paying support for him until the need for repairs, new shoes, or anything else arose. I felt he needed to know. I made it known that support for me wasn't where I drew the line and that I would come out of my pocket for whatever was needed for my children. I also made it known that because of the unnecessary game playing, I would not allow anyone to use or mishandle me. He was old enough to hear truths, straight with no chaser. It was awful after our getting connected because the things he endured by being constantly thrown in the middle were just heartbreaking.

Each opportunity that came about to stay in my pockets, I shut it down. My son's car broke down in the middle of the street one day around the corner from his friend's father's house. He called me as I was out running errands. Once I arrived, his friend's dad had already helped him get it to the front of his home.

I met the friend's father who, like the other friend's mother, didn't know who my son's parents were, was very nice and generous to lend a hand in telling me what was wrong with the car. I thanked him for allowing us to leave the car in front of his house until my son could get it towed.

When we left and were on our way to take him home, I had him call home to report what happened and that I was dropping him off. During this call, as he was explaining the situation, he said that he needed to get it towed to a shop and our son asked him how he was going to do this and how was he going to afford to get it taken care of? Our son had a part-time job, and was using his checks to take care of the car's expenses and whatever else he may have wanted for himself without help. I later learned I was to pick up the financial slack.

As he was face timing, he was asked, "Who are you with?"

He said, "Mom."

Then he said, "Exactly."

So that's when I finally, for the first time in a long time, spoke up. "No. I'm bringing him home to you so you can take care of it and help pay for it because if you need my help, you receive it already monthly, so use it. You will not keep slick taking advantage of me, so handle it!"

There were minor words exchanged between us, which felt foreign, as we had not verbalized with each other in over five years. It was sad but necessary. In the end, he handled it without my being involved.

The asking and message relaying stopped from my son over things needed. When he'd asked me for something he wanted, I did it, no questions asked. I chalked it up to the fact that this wasn't a competition of who could do what and nothing was being taken from me I wasn't willing to give.

He would soon graduate from high school a year early and entering the United States Navy. All that mattered to me was to appreciate the time I had with him, make as many memories as I could, and not dwell on the negativity. Yes, I was a little down. I felt my time with him was stolen and now he was moving right along. However, I had a hand in it, too, by the decisions I'd made. I needed to keep grounded so I could enjoy what God gave back to me, so I did. I had my daughter back a little before our son was to leave as time winded down and I was good. We were good.

All in all, my son dealt with a lot before graduating and leaving for the military. It was hard to witness without coming out of a bag over him going through unnecessary things because of the hearts of man. To forgive is epic because it changed my heart. No matter what was thrown my way, I buried the old me and who I am now will continue to show up instead of showing out. Besides, all that chaos is exhausting.

CHAPTER SEVENTEEN

Whole Healing

Since COVID-19, it was hard for some to be on "lockdown" and easy for others. My son was a senior who couldn't go to his prom. He had to finish out the school year via online classes. Cancellation of the normal school dances given at the end of each school year. He didn't have those senior memories he could hold dear for a lifetime. Because of COVID, he did not experience what everyone in the country experiences, his first graduation. Because of being on lockdown, he had to stop working his job. It also cut down on our being able to see each other for a long while. It was hard. To know fault of his own, it caused major issues. His presence was doable when he was working, going to school, and not always around. He was being tolerated because of having to be home daily. Our children told me about how she treated them while they were overseas and how she'd put on airs in front of others as though showering them with love. When you add others to a circle, a situation can be a beautiful outcome or a not-so-beautiful one. What's in the heart of a man creates the atmosphere. This is what God showed me about myself, as well as others.

Whatever is inside, no matter how you disguise it or drape it with immaculate garments, eventually, the truth will appear on the outside. It is hard to hide who we really are because the truth is inevitable.

As my son was visiting with me, his stepmother demanded that he come home (forty-five minutes away) to clean the bathroom. I told my son, "As if and I wish you would." That was not happening, even if he wanted to go take care of it. Another occasion was when he was at home doing online schooling and didn't take out the trash pettiness reared its ugly head again and he was being provoked then she stopped speaking to him. My son stopped communication with her, saying he just obliged and went along. He'd grown these beautiful locks in his hair and when he needed them redone, he asked about it and was told, "Oh, so now you are talking?" I just told him to come over so I could do them for him instead. It was difficult to witness such immaturity and could do nothing about it. My son simply wanted to get through his senior year so he could fly on his own. I felt bad for him. Without even trying, he wound up in the middle of a one-sided war. You can't go to battle over a reason you know nothing about. I wasn't in a war. Those days were long gone, so what was happening during this time was unacceptable, but was taking place with no real reasoning.

Now that he couldn't work or go to school, he stayed in like he was supposed to do. He was constantly being picked with and discomforted by pestering him about not being able to go to work and small petty things. It tore me up when he'd call and I'd hear the hurt and what felt like him being bullied and couldn't fight back in his voice. It got to where I couldn't watch him going through it because he has always been a good kid and I knew without having to make excuses for him; he wasn't doing anything to cause this treatment. He started being cursed at and talked down to, to the point of him coming to stay with me. When he came, he told me all that had gone on and that he didn't want to be there and couldn't wait to graduate and leave.

He stayed for a while and went back. I understood because all his things were there and in a situation like that to where you must pack some parts of you in bags and leave the other parts in another place wasn't easy. I've been there before. Going back wasn't the first choice. He wasn't back long before he called me at five-thirty in the morning to tell me that, out of nowhere, she stormed into his room and took his cords to his XBOX game. He said he got up and asked why they were being taken as at the time he wasn't asleep and was talking to his friends on his phone, which was clearly noted. He didn't get an answer, so he asked again and was told to back off before he got knocked out. When he tried to plead his case and he wanted his cords back, he was told, "Just ride it out." This was because he was soon leaving for the military. My son said that he would not ride it out and was leaving. Yes, this was difficult for me to hear and not get involved, but I maintained on my square.

He stayed with me for a long while this time and then had to see his recruiter, so he had to go back home for a day and stayed the night. He called me and stated that he wasn't even back for a whole two hours and again, things started in on him when he did nothing to cause the behavior. Yes, I took one foot off my square but put it back because I realized it wasn't about my son at all. So, I stood firm on my square and prayed for the household whenever my son had to be in it. My son had plans to go to community school first before joining the military so he could enter at a higher rank. However, he said, "Mom, I'm just ready to go." I told him to do what he felt he needed to do, but to make sure it was what he wanted to do. Different things happened during this time, like when my daughter finished with AmeriCorp and had to deal with similar mistreatment.

Every tax refund I received, I paid toward child support arrears, along with the regular monthly payments. However, I'd received yet another summons from the court of child support to add my son to my health insurance. Mind you, he was getting ready to graduate high school and go to the military. He would have his own insurance. Plus, it would emancipate him and he could start taking care of himself. Now, I was already paying child support in the state where I live. He filed for child support in another state, which was the forty-five-minute distance he lived in across lines into another state. So, not only was I paying in my state, I had started receiving a coupon book from the other state, too. He assumed he could file in two states because he *assumed* I lacked knowledge of the process. I called this support agency in the other state to make them aware of my paying where I lived. The agency contacted my home state for confirmation. They were supposed to have noted this, but it never dropped. It ended up on my credit report as though I paid no support at all. I had to fight to prove my case and to get them to remove it from my credit. Then this summons arrived out of the blue.

Not only was I working hard at staying healthy during this season from being an essential worker, but I had to deal with what didn't even make sense. Why was coming for me still important and being the number one focus? I just didn't get it.

It was hard not to lash out, but I'd grown so much that I had to deal with my spiritual warfare with my adversary and win it. I had to. I needed to. There was so much more that was important to me.

Upon my son leaving for boot camp, he told me he would bring me his enlistment papers so I could send them to the Child Support Agency to prove his emancipation. He also brought his diploma for me to send as well. I sent a letter and the attachments to the other state, letting them know I was not supposed to pay in their state. I let them know what happened and why they placed me in their system. The agency received my papers. They said they would close my case and once it was closed, it would come off my credit. I was told to keep monitoring this so that it would become a reality, which was fine with me. I called the agency in my home state. I wanted to know my next step and how much I was in arrears. She stated my case there would be closed as well upon receiving all the paperwork I'd sent to them with the copy of the letter written to the other agency. She also told me that of the $10,000 I was in arrears, I only owed $591.00 and to not pay it out of pocket because the support would continue coming out of my pay until the case was closed at the end of the next month. Once it was closed, I could then find out the rest that was left and pay it off. *Hallelujah!*

All the years of turmoil and bullying that turned into strength, growth, looking past slick jabs, and having my life back with no subpoenas had manifested. It was finally over. Things could have been different. We could have had conversations on an adult level to where everyone in the circle could have made things work for two precious souls that never asked for any of the dysfunction. The joy wasn't over. I was no longer paying the support, which meant no longer having that connection. The chain was broken and I could breathe no matter what other issues arose. I didn't have to utter a word, see any more ill facial expressions, or anything of the sort. It was over.

Knowing there won't be any more headaches nor looking around the corner for the next episode of entitlements seemed unbelievable. Even in my angriest moments, I felt I couldn't get any more hurt, and it was always a new way that broke through what I felt was my worse. I always thought, *Lord, when is it going to stop, and me and the kids can just live?* All the calls, after the initial anger, I tried to make to become civil, which made me look weak, intimidated, and soft…I thought would work.

Being questioned why I thought my way would work when it was consistently plain that I was beating my head against a brick wall. Questions like, was I still in love with him as to the reason I didn't get grimy and low down as he was getting with me. Still, I kept holding onto what I needed to have some type of stability in our children's lives, after seeing their faces during the instability. It was hard and yes, I slipped into my own exhausting feelings and spoke how I was feeling. This proved nothing but caused more hurt not only in my heart but in the kids' as well.

Being apart from my children was difficult. I held my own scavenger hunts, looking for anything that reminded me of them. Searching for pictures of them on social media. It all was futile, however. I just wanted a glimpse of them. Anything. Day in and day out, searching for that smallest glimpse of treasure in hopes to find something I could hold on to—a smile, a frown, a pose, an event they had attended. In my search and once I could see them on their Instagram pages, I'd search each of their pages until I'd find something and I'd have to screenshot it.

Posting pictures of them on my Facebook page and Instagram of things I wasn't even a part of made me somehow feel as though I was a fraud. I was the mother, and I had to steal memories that I couldn't be a part of. As if I were screenshotting pictures of kids I barely knew. The thought of it; I could feel the warmth creeping up my neck and the lump in my throat. It was crazy.

It broke my heart to learn from other people, who had seen pictures, that my daughter went to her senior prom. They told me how beautiful she was and how nice her dress was, taking me back to when the wives in military housing would say, "Isn't it nice that the ship came back early?" It dumbfounded me to receive that information but I had to play it off to not feel some type of way to the person who relayed the information.

The person who told me about her dress sent me a picture. I don't remember how long I cried, but I did and posted it. I posted something that I had no hand in. Her dress was beautiful, her makeup, her hair, and she even had on heels. This ripped my heart out with hurt and happiness all at once. I needed that moment in her life. I needed to be the one to talk to her while helping her with her makeup and fixing her hair. I needed that. Wow, the many mother/daughter moments that were snatched away were the same moments I gave away without thinking it totally through. I watched my children grow through pictures and had to piece them together.

When she graduated from high school in Japan, it was the most hurtful event and the enemy even used this as a pawn in sickness. It was already bad enough that I could not be there to cheer her on and scream, "That's my baby up there!"

My daughter had told me that if I wanted to come to her graduation, that *he* would buy the tickets for me to come. I couldn't express my true feelings to my daughter regarding the offer so I told her I was so deeply sorry that I couldn't be there but know that my heart, kisses, hugs, and spirit were there with her more than she would ever know.

The sad thing is that the undermined offer was an attempt to show that he made an effort to help me be a part of things, and I declined. Why would I accept tickets from the same people who wished me ill and put me in harm's way? Why would I go on the other side of the world alone, with nowhere to stay and be at the mercy of my adversaries? Really?

So, I resumed what had become my norm, sifting through their online pictures of different events. I took screenshots of her participation in different groups like the clubs she'd joined and events like high school rallies, games, etc. Crying became a thorn in my side but venting became exhausting to those who weren't walking in my shoes. So, with God's help, I survived through it all.

I learned that my son was running track. I never saw him run in a meet or have pictures I would have taken had I been present. I took screenshots of him and his friends when I could catch it.

It was just a horrible scene altogether, but without the endurance through Him keeping me, I couldn't have made it and, now it's over. I have had to swallow large pills that were hard to keep down. I discovered all we go through isn't because of who we are or what we did. Happenstances happen with no warning, with some of them being extraordinary to events extremely toxic. God never said life would be easy. I thank Him for trusting me with all I've faced. I thank Him for believing I would handle it the way He orchestrated me to in my heart. He trusted me. Many times I knew this and fought to not disappoint.

I'm thankful that I built my relationship with Christ and not depend on my outlook on how things should be by implementing my personal plans. Marriage meant a lot to me and I honored it as I should have and our children added a completion to the circle that was astronomical in my eyes and heart. I lived and breathed my circle. I also lived, breathed, and felt the weight of all the chains after the circle was broken.

After all the madness, someone had to stop and grow up, so I walked away years ago from any type of hatred, bitterness, and unforgiveness. My sanity was at stake. Getting reconnected with my children was at stake. I was getting older and wiser and wanted complete healing. I would not win by cheating the system and lying, so even if most times it felt like I was losing and looked the same, I had to hold on.

It was over and I was free. I cried one night after it was all confirmed that child support was over, arrears were over, court was over, having had to feel like at one point I needed to prove the lies talked about me were untrue and hidden sucker punches were over. Trying to keep both feet on my square without springing off into a matrix position was a challenge in not responding to a lot of things that were done toward me. It was over.

When it was time for my son to leave for the military, plans were made, without his permission, for him to spend time with the other side of the family, leaving no time for my son to spend with me. He also wanted to spend some time with his friends before leaving, so his window of time was tight. So, my son, bless his heart, has always been the peacekeeper and respectful. He spent time with me once I got off work and we talked about a lot of things with my pouring into him what I could before he left because I knew I wouldn't get to see him again before leaving for boot camp. I cried after he left for reasons only me and God could understand without my having to rehash past situations. I was proud of my son for trying his best to do the right thing, as it is what I raised them both to do no matter what or who was doing the wrong. I was and am so proud of them both.

With both of my children now living their lives as adults in this huge world away from me, I pray they do great on their journeys through life. My daughter is bright, intelligent, and knows what she wants out of life. She is such a trooper and survivor and I admire her so much. I'm happy to have her back in my life and that she is just a phone call and a visit away now. I pray my son learns from the experience within his circle of family to know the difference in transparency, love, and forgiveness. I pray for much success over their lives and for a sound mind in decision-making. My son and I talked about what he was expecting once he arrived at boot camp, how it might be, and all the people from all over the world that he was going to meet. He also talked about the car he wanted to buy, where he wanted to go for his first tour, and other things. When it was time for him to go, we hugged so tight that the strongest person couldn't pry us apart. He hugged me so tight that I felt all that he wanted to say and then some. Then he told me how much he loved me and was going to miss me. I silently prayed over him while we embraced and he kissed me on the cheek and said again, "I love you, Mom." I returned the gesture and watched him walk out of the door and my heart sunk. I wasn't ready to let him go again.

I've learned that no one can control what anyone else does or how the heart pumps. I've learned that you must allow people to have their feelings because it only affects you with your permission. Where there is unhappiness, actions follow and all you can do is pray over it, be thankful that it is not your story, and continue living. The last and final jab toward me was when it was time for my son to graduate boot camp. Because of the pandemic, no one could go to see him graduate. If it were possible, I would have been there with bells and whistles, but it was not. So, when I spoke with him, he'd stated that he had his graduation pictures with him in his uniform and other pictures for me and my mother along with a shadow box he specifically made for me but the military had to send all the pictures taken to the address listed on his records. It wasn't my address, so I immediately felt that I would never receive my pictures.

I was right. To this day, I've never received my son's military pictures after he was promised I would get them through my daughter who was now living on her own. She was to bring them to me and for months was given different dates and times to come to pick them up, but each time she attempted to retrieve them, something happened to where she couldn't get them. Finally, when she went to get them, she was told that they would not give them to her and that if I wanted them, I would have to come to get them myself. It was just never-ending and sad that things couldn't be different.

With this, I told my daughter to take herself out of the middle and I would be okay. I wasn't okay, though. Not only had I had to pretend I was a part of their lives through stealing pictures off their social media now, what was meant for me was not relinquished. I was angry, and hurt, knowing that hatred is a sickness and I wanted no part of such a thing. There is no trust there. Going to pick up pictures from the character traits I've experienced would have been like going to see my children upon returning from overseas and having the police to escort me off the property. These were known actions, so trusting that this was an option was a no-go. If maturity and civility were the initial position, we would have never gone through a lot of things, so I sent a text that read, *Keep the pictures, if it makes you feel as though there is power you hold in doing it. Obviously, there is a need to see me but I am uninterested and it won't happen so keep what you stole just like everything else. Be Blessed.*

All I can do is wait for my son to return home and hopefully I will receive them then. I had to swallow yet another one of those large pills and move on. Acting on the same level would not prove anything, and learning this very thing had taught me everything. I know what my son looks like and even though I can only imagine how handsome he looked in his pictures and my mother wasn't able to receive the ones that were sent for her as well, we had to chalk it up. We had to pray for the less fortunate in character. It is all you can do. Some things you just can't fix.

Still, everything had ended and I honestly didn't know how to feel. I felt relieved, sad, happy, and grateful. My children and I are survivors and with the help of Jesus, we made it through the tough times when it overshadowed the good times. When things are stolen from our journeys and plans, nothing good comes from it so I accepted things as they were. I didn't need it to make sense to anyone else. My conversations with my Father confirmed all that He was doing and still doing up to this point.

He has provided healing from the pain and disappointments. He taught me forgiveness no matter how hard it may be to do because it's not about the other person but about an individual growth that surpasses all that it looks like to the naked eye. It's freedom.

Leaving a marriage isn't a cakewalk. It's death. No one marries with the plans drawn up for the "just in cases" outside of those who believe in prenuptial marriages. When my divorce was final after years of separation, it was to be just that. I wasn't allowed to grieve, go through the burial of it, take time to find myself, heal and deal with acceptance. I couldn't move on with my life and find my happy. I had to fight to get to a point of sanity that always lasted temporarily upon the next cyclone that would habitually touch down. It has taken a long, long time to reach my rationality in things. Living life is balance, maturation, trusting in the process of footsteps taken, and learning from each step to not repeat them through experience. Life is deciding to breathe when you're put in a situation that might alter the airflow. I'm still breathing.

Today I'm a new creature. The scars from yesterday are visible in some places and some wounds are still open slightly, but the sting is gone. Scars that were once weak and timid are now an ironclad of strength. I don't play with yesterday nor give it my time. My journey getting to today was long and brutal, so I cherish it with everything I am. That word *peace* has been so irresponsibly handled throughout my life. Today, it's my absolute best friend and we understand each other's mojo now. Peace speaks to me and lets me know when it is being tested and tried. Once it communicates the discomfort to me, I spring into action to make sure we remain in alignment. It is the one thing that regardless of anything that is transpiring around me, I won't compromise. It cost too much to devalue and mishandle.

I have the benefit of hearing from God. He clears paths to which way I am to go in life. He gives solid warnings. I may think about my yesterday for a hot minute, which is about as long as it lasts.

Today I have the gift of goodbye and am anointed with the word, "No." Today, self-love comes before protecting another's wrongful approach or distasteful gestures. To be unbothered does not mean to be uncaring. It means you place things, people, issues in their proper order.

I had to learn how to kill my flesh to grow. I don't mind saying that I slept with one of those long body pillows to suffice sleeping next to someone. Sometimes, I'd have to sleep with smaller pillows between my thighs to suppress my urges to be with someone. Being completely transparent, I couldn't sleep sometimes because my flesh craved a release. I'd chosen to listen to the voice of the Holy Spirit to fall in love and love myself with no validation. I needed to get back to me.

It took a long time to learn to be with just me. It was doable and necessary to break free from the distractions. I was ready to focus to gain clarity of what God had laid out just for me to execute.

Yes, I get lonely, but the value of my worth, and the journey I traveled to get here, negotiating just to have someone isn't an option. One day I will find love and I am open to it, but I will be fine if it doesn't happen. I'm not unrealistically inclined to believe there will be no storms and trials. When two people get together, they are not the same. They are individuals with their own ways of thinking, differences in opinions, and perspectives. As I've gotten older and through experiences of my own mistakes made in the dos and don'ts department, I'll know how to weather the storms because I won't be choosing who to be with by myself the next time around. I'll have a Father to go to for wisdom before leaping.

God didn't intend for us to be alone, but it's not always defined as being married or in a relationship. Along the way, I've learned that marriage is a ministry, and He doesn't take it lightly. If it is to be a part of my ministry ever again, I'll know. I've also learned that being single is not a disease or a phase. It's a choice and the defining of my singleness goes beyond self-love. It is clarity, it is happy, it is the freedom to simply be, it is friendships, it is adventures, and it is a conversation. It is *peace*.

Today I can breathe and exhale while loving on me and stepping into my purpose. I am better so that I can be someone else's better. I'll know how to love, listen, laugh, understand the difference in picking a battle over solving one, complimenting the atmosphere instead of complicating it, and communicating. Oh, she ready! I put God first, therefore nothing is impossible.

The stench of my yesterday does not have power over my today. I continue to pray that one day the hard heartened will see God and learn that living in a room full of coal will continue to leave clouds of darkness and soot. I pray that healing and forgiveness will come.

I'm past my fears of hurting other people's feelings at the expense of my own. I did this a lot and there is a way to be honest and respectful. I'm past sugar coating truth at the expense of my own truths. I'm past compromising what I know would present itself as a detonator if given the room as small as a slither of leeway into my life. I'm past allowing the naysayers' words to find a home in my heart or mind. I'm past not owning my strength in fear of downplaying another's strength. I'm past it.

My heart is finally reflecting what was deposited from the beginning. *Me!* I earned my spot, and I fought like a champ and won every heavyweight champion belt that victory would allow. I took the punches of degradation, mistreatment, backbiting, humiliation, manipulation, soiled leftovers concerning the matters of the heart and had to fight out of the corner like a shivering dog. I handled the tight, swollen, and painful eyes from crying repeatedly over what ended up making me stronger than I could ever imagine.

I walk with my head up because I am a Queen, a King's kid, highly favored, covered, and blessed! I get to empower someone else with my story and how I made it through to my today.

Today, I smile. I could have stayed broken, but I didn't. What was broken has mended and what was brutalized, I gave Him room to overpower the power I allowed others to have unworthily that shook my confidence. My heart smiles because my children survived in a world of manipulation, my anger, other's anger, mistakes made, all the while searching for some type of stability amid the nightmare. They got to see both sides. They upheld their sanity when I know it was difficult to do.

I know what it feels like to have a story that is so long and drawn out that fear sets in and you bury it. I'd buried this too long already in fear of retribution. How long was I to keep things in and continue to allow people to cause destruction, pain, dismantle hearts, lies, paint a picture that wasn't real and get to walk away as if I deserved what happened and everyone simply had to get over it?

Writing this book years after I'd endured so much has not been a walk in the park. However, today, I'm lifted and empowered. The shackles around my ankles are off and now I dance in my shoes. I'm loving my today.

Remember in all things, no matter how long the storm seems to last, keep the faith. Weeping endures for a night (sometimes, it endures for many nights), but *joy* will come in the morning.

About the Author

A native of Chicago, Illinois, Kimberly Blake is the founder and CEO of Adored Sistahs & Young Sistah Power, an organization for empowering and uplifting women of all ages and through all stages of life, including her twenty-three-year-old daughter. Having experienced a variety of life's lessons in womanhood, motherhood of two thriving young adults, she has found her purpose in paying it forward through writing, inspiring, and sharing her walk with Christ, which is the best relationship she's ever had.

Through her organization, Kim reaches the masses with truth, information, and the love she's found within herself. She has not only discovered how self-love impacts and opens so many doors regarding the treatment of others and treatments received, but self-stewardship over the gifts, talents, and heart that God created in her from the very beginning. If she can place the smallest glimpse of what a renewed mindset can do in a person's life, then she has achieved what she has set out to do—to prove that anything is possible if you believe.

Currently working on her next literary work, Kim lives in San Antonio, Texas.

Follow her on social media:
Facebook: Kimberly Blake/Adored Sistahs & Young Sistah Power
Instagram: Kimblake50